With the
compliments
of the
Canada Council

Avec les
hommages
du Conseil des
Arts du Canada

Canadian War Museum

Historical Publications Number 5

Editor: John Swettenham
        Curator, Historical Resources

[1] *Canada and the First World War*, John Swettenham, English and French (Canadian War Museum, 1968).

[2] *D-Day*, John Swettenham, English and French (Canadian War Museum, 1969).

[3] *Canada and the First World War*, John Swettenham, based on the 50th Anniversary Armistice Display at the Canadian War Museum, profusely illustrated (Ryerson, 1969).

[4] *Canadian Military Aircraft*, J. A. Griffin, English and French (Queen's Printer, 1969).

The Canadian War Museum is part of the National Museum of Man, National Museums of Canada.

The

Last

War Drum

The North West Campaign
of 1885

HAKKERT, TORONTO
1972

Desmond Morton

The

Last

War Drum

This book has been published with the help of a grant
from the Social Science Research Council of Canada
using funds provided by the Canada Council.

Standard Book Number: 88866-512-1

Library of Congress Catalogue Card Number: 72-80054

A. M. Hakkert Ltd.
554 Spadina Crescent
Toronto 179, Canada

Printed in Canada

to David and Marion

Someday they will
have to understand

Foreword

The North-West campaign of 1885 arose from the first major crisis to face the young Dominion of Canada. The circumstances which led to Louis Riel's challenge to Canadian sovereignty in the North-West involved issues which are still very much part of the fabric of political controversy in Canada. The relations of French- and English-speaking Canadians, the future place of the Indian in a predominantly white society, the complex basis for Western alienation from Canada as a whole—these are problems which more than a century of Confederation has yet to solve.

If the issues of 1885 seem familiar, the actual military operations of the 1885 campaign are much less well known. Yet the courage and endurance which both sides displayed, the dilemmas which faced the leaders, deserve to be better appreciated by Canadians.

1885 heard the last war drum sound in Canada. It was the last, desperate chance for Indians and Metis to impose their own terms on the settlement of the West. It was also, in a dozen practical ways, our "first war." Apart from the valued services of a few British officers, the 1885 campaign was the first military undertaking in which Canadians were virtually on their own. Not only was it necessary to mobilize a field army from the untrained and ill-equipped Canadian militia, it was necessary to improvise transport, supply and medical services to allow the force to move and survive.

Somehow, it was accomplished. From this achievement, Canadians began to acquire the practical experience and the self-confidence which could form the basis for our national military tradition and heritage.

The author of this study, Desmond Morton, is a professor of Canadian history at the University of Toronto. A graduate of the Royal Military College, Kingston, of Oxford University and the London School of Economics, he was also a soldier and a descendant of a family of soldiers who have served Canada in almost all our campaigns. One of his ancestors, General Sir William Otter, played his own prominent role in the events of 1885.

Lee F. Murray
Curator
Canadian War Museum

Acknowledgements

My original incentive for examining the 1885 campaign was a task, shared with Professor R. H. Roy of the University of Victoria, of preparing an edition of the telegrams exchanged between Sir Adolphe Caron, the Minister of Militia, and officers and officials in the North-West during the 1885 rebellion. I gratefully acknowledge the benefits of collaborating with Professor Roy and with Professor Morris Zaslow, the editor for the Champlain Society. I have also profited from the advice of Dr. P. M. Eisner.

Much of the research for this study was done at the Public Archives of Canada in Ottawa and at the Toronto Reference Library. It has been greatly assisted by the knowledge and kindness of the staff of both of these institutions. Like almost all others who have ever worked in Canadian military history, I owe an enormous debt to Colonel Charles Stacey, former director of the Army Historical Section and now a colleague at the University of Toronto. His fund of encouragement and constructive guidance has been replenished by his successor, Professor S. F. Wise, and other members of the staff of the Canadian Forces Historical Section. Like anyone who ventures into the 1885 period, I am also the debtor of a former teacher, Professor G. F. G. Stanley, formerly Dean of Arts at the Royal Military College and now at Mount Allison University in Sackville, New Brunswick.

Without the encouragement of John Swettenham, senior historian of the Canadian War Museum and without his editorial assistance and the help of other former colleagues, Frank McGuire and Fred Azar, this book would never have appeared. For the virtues of the book, they deserve full credit; for its faults, the author is fully to blame.

Illustrations for the book have been made available largely through the courtesy of the Public Archives of Canada and the Archives of Manitoba. Maps, based on contemporary sketches and plans, were prepared by Mrs. Georgie Anderson and Mrs. Mabel Riendeau and Mr. Steve Jaunszems assisted with the photography. Financial assistance for this study was forthcoming through a research grant from the Canada Council while help in obtaining the illustrations was provided by the Learning Media Committee of Erindale College, University of Toronto. Publication has been made possible through a grant from the Social Science Research Council.

Above all, I must acknowledge the long forbearance and substantial practical assistance of my wife, Janet. Few people could have stood—and understood—so much.

Desmond Morton
Mississauga,
September, 1972

Table of Contents

The Last War Drum

List of Illustrations and Maps

Pictures

Maps

Picture Credits:

J. W. Bengough, *Grip,* pp. 15, 138, 148, 152, 159, 162.
British Columbia Archives, 26.
Manitoba Archives, 45.
Otter Collection, cover, 30, 34, 100, 102.
Public Archies of Canada, iv, v, xiv, xvi-xvii, xix, xxii, 2, 4, 6, 7, 9, 11, 12, 13, 17, 18, 19,
    20, 22, 27, 29, 31, 32, 34, 35, 36, 39, 40, 41, 42, 46, 48, 50, 52, 54, 55, 56-7, 59, 60, 62,
    63, 64, 66, 67, 70, 72, 74, 76, 77, 79, 80, 81, 82-3, 84, 85, 86, 88, 89, 90, 91, 92, 93, 96,
    98, 101, 105, 106-7, 108, 109, 114, 115, 116-7, 119, 120, 122, 124, 128, 129, 130, 131,
    132, 134, 135, 136, 139, 140-1, 142, 143, 146, 150, 154, 155, 157, 161, 163, 164-5, 166,
    168.
Royal Ontario Museum, 4.
T. B. Strange, *Gunner Jingo's Jubilee,* 113, 121.

What did the Privates do?

(To the tune of "Solomon Levi")

Our dailies team with daring deeds,
And books are filled with fame,
Brass bands will play and cannons roar
In honour of the name,
Of men who held commissions, and
Were honest, brave and true,
But still the question comes to me,
WHAT DID THE PRIVATES DO?

Who were the men to guard the camp
When the foes were hovering round?
Who dug the graves of comrades dear?
Who laid them in the ground?
Who sent the dying message home
To those he never knew?
If officers did all of this,
WHAT DID THE PRIVATES DO?

Who were the men to fill the place
Of comrades killed in strife?
Who were the men to risk their own
To save a comrade's life?
Who was it lived on salted pork
And bread too hard to chew?
If Officers did this alone
WHAT DID THE PRIVATES DO?

Who laid in pits on rainy nights
All eager for the fray
Who marched beneath a scorching sun
Through many a toilsome day?
Who paid the sutler double price
And scanty rations drew?
If officers get all the praise
THEN, WHAT DID THE PRIVATES DO?

All honor to the brave, wild boys,
Who rallied at the call –
Without regard to name or rank
We honor one & all
They're passing over one by one
And soon they'll all be gone
To where the books will surely show
Just what the boys have done.

from: Sir William Otter Papers, Staff Diary 1885

Chronology

July 1, 1867	The three provinces of Canada, Nova Scotia and New Brunswick enter Confederation under the British North America Act.
December 1, 1869	Louis Riel proclaims his "List of Grievances" and emerges as the dominant figure in a provisional government for the Red River colony.
March 4, 1870	At Riel's insistence, Thomas Scott is shot outside the walls of Fort Garry.
May 12, 1870	The Manitoba Act receives Royal assent, adding a fifth province to the Dominion of Canada.
July 15, 1870	The vast domain of the Hudson's Bay Company is formally annexed to the Dominion as its North-West Territories.
July 8, 1874	The North-West Mounted Police, three hundred strong, sets out from Fort Dufferin to extend Canadian authority across the Territories.
June 15, 1875	The Earl of Dufferin personally exercises the vice-regal prerogative of mercy for the last time by commuting the death sentence on Ambrose Lepine, Riel's adjutant-general, in 1870.
October 21, 1880	The Dominion government signs a contract with the Canadian Pacific Railway Company to complete a transcontinental railway.
June 5, 1884	Louis Riel agrees to accompany a half-breed delegation back to Saskatchewan.

December 16, 1884   A petition drafted by Riel, expressing the grievances of the Indians and Métis, is forwarded to Ottawa.

February 4, 1885   The Minister of the Interior informs the Lieutenant Governor of the North-West Territories that the government will investigate half-breed claims to land grants and titles.

March 18-19, 1885   Riel seizes hostages at Batoche and proclaims a new Métis provisional government, with Gabriel Dumont as his adjutant general.

March 26, 1885   Superintendent Crozier rides out to meet the defiance of government authority and is badly defeated in a clash at Duck Lake.

April 1, 1885   Nine whites and half-breeds are murdered by Crees of Big Bear's band at Frog Lake.

April 6, 1885   Major General Middleton leaves Fort Qu'Appelle with the first available troops to march to Clarke's Crossing and Batoche.

April 11, 1885   Lieutenant Colonel Otter's column is diverted to the relief of police and settlers at Battleford.

April 15, 1885   Inspector Dickens abandons Fort Pitt after the white civilians under his protection decide to surrender to Big Bear.

April 25, 1885   Part of Middleton's column meets Dumont at Fish Creek in the first major battle of the campaign. Colonel Otter's column enters Battleford.

May 3, 1885   Otter's attack on Poundmaker's camp at Cut Knife fails and the Canadians withdraw to Battleford.

May 6, 1885   The steamer *Northcote* reaches Clarke's Crossing.

May 9-12, 1885   Middleton's column reaches Batoche and engages in a four-day battle, culminating in a successful assault on the Métis settlement.

May 15, 1885   Riel surrenders to Middleton's scouts.

May 25, 1885   Poundmaker surrenders to Middleton near Battleford.

May 27, 1885   General Strange fights an inconclusive battle with Big Bear's men at Frenchman's Butte.

June 3, 1885   Middleton starts on the pursuit of Big Bear.

June 9, 1885   Middleton at Loon Lake abandons the pursuit.

July 2, 1885   Big Bear arrives at Fort Carlton to surrender.

August 1, 1885   After a trial for high treason at Regina, Riel is found guilty and sentenced to be hanged.

November 16, 1885   Louis Riel is hanged at the police barracks in Regina.

The

Last

War Drum

Gabriel Dumont, Riel's adjutant general. A shrewd, courageous fighter, he had one fatal military weakness; he subordinated his military judgement to Riel's.

I. Duck Lake

Early on a bitterly cold Thursday morning, March 26th, 1885, a little force of North West Mounted Police and civilians rode up the steep bank behind the ramshackle trading post at Fort Carlton. Then, horses' nostrils steaming in the frost, they turned south, heading along the snowy trail that led to Duck Lake. Nearby was Hillyard Mitchell's store; inside was food and other supplies, perhaps also arms and ammunition.

Only a week before, the police had been faced with a blunt and brutal challenge. On behalf of his newly created provisional government, Louis Riel had promised "a war of extermination upon all those who have shown themselves hostile to our rights." The alternative was the immediate surrender of the police at Carlton and Battleford. Such threats could hardly be expected to cow Superintendent Leif Crozier, commanding "D" Division. The summer before at Battleford, outnumbered and threatened by furious Indians, he had coolly and firmly arrested the suspected assailants of a white farm instructor. Now, still the symbol and substance of Canadian authority on the North Saskatchewan, the police would put Riel's bold words to the test. The little party heading for Mitchell's store would discover whether the Métis leader was prepared to exercise his proclaimed authority. Riel was.

Three miles from their destination, the small group of police and civilians reined in their horses to face a much larger band of mounted Métis whose leader was Gabriel Dumont, a burly former buffalo hunter, the newly appointed Adjutant General in Riel's provisional government. There were threats, jeers, a demand that the police party surrender. A shot was fired. Fearing a trap, the police wheeled about and withdrew, mustering all the dignity their discomfiture would allow. Meanwhile, a messenger raced ahead to Fort Carlton, carrying the news.

For a man like Superintendent Crozier there was only one possible response. The authority of the Force had been challenged; defiance had to be met by prompt, decisive action. It was the answer his men had

The battle near Duck Lake. Caught in the open, Crozier's men were easy targets for Métis and Indians shrewdly concealed behind cover.

expected and wanted. Within an hour, Crozier was on the trail to Duck Lake, leading fifty-two police and forty-three white settlers from Prince Albert, sworn in as special constables. Some were mounted, most were packed on horse-drawn sleighs. With them came a venerable seven-pounder cannon, specially mounted on a winter carriage.

A mile and a half from Mitchell's store, Crozier met the Métis. There were more of them now, with Indians and Riel himself to reinforce their numbers. Hurriedly, the police and volunteers dismounted, dragging their sleighs into a barricade across the trail, while Crozier went forward to talk. He was met by Dumont's brother, Isidore, and an Indian. While they argued with increasing anger on both sides, Dumont's men slipped into a wooded depression which commanded one flank of the police position. Others occupied an abandoned log hut which overlooked the other flank. By now, Crozier's interpreter was struggling to wrest his gun away from the Indian; and Crozier realized that he was soon to be surrounded. A shot resounded, the Indian fell, and a volley came from the police barricade. It was immediately returned as Métis poured in fire from three sides. The police cannon boomed off a few ineffective rounds and fell silent. A panic-stricken gunner had loaded the ball before the charge.

For half an hour, police and volunteers lay almost helpless under a murderous rain of bullets. The volunteers, exposed and ill-prepared, suffered most. With the three other officers either dead or wounded, himself bleeding from a wound on his cheek, Crozier reluctantly ordered a retreat. Somehow the sleighs were turned, terrified horses were coaxed into the traces and most of the wounded were piled aboard. As the survivors headed back along the trail to Carlton, the Métis fire slackened. Bearing only a crucifix, Louis Riel rushed out in the snow: "For the love of God, don't kill any more. There's too much blood spilled already." The firing stopped.[1]

And blood there was. Nine of Crozier's men lay dead in the snow. Another, severely wounded, was only just saved from death at the hands of the Indians. Five horses, three sleighs and a dozen rifles had been abandoned. Total casualties among the ninety-five police and civilians in Crozier's force were twelve killed and eleven wounded. However, it had cost the Métis and Indians five of their own lives to demolish the police legend of invincibility. Dumont himself was wounded and his brother, Isidore, lay among the dead. Moreover, the triumph was not complete. It had been an essential part of Riel's strategy to seize Crozier and his men as hostages: his own intervention at the end of the engagement had ensured their escape. The fight would now be continued.[2]

Duck Lake was both an end and a beginning. The shots which began the last, desperate struggle of the Métis people and their Indian allies also ended the interminably slow and faulty process by which the Canadian government had sought, since 1870, to evolve an acceptable basis of existence for the indigenous people of the North-West.

• • •

If there was any single, fresh common purpose among the political leaders of the three colonies of British North America who united in 1867 to create the Dominion of Canada, it was to lay hands on the great, empty region of the North-West, to ensure that their new nation would live up to her new motto and extend "from sea unto sea." Silent on so many crucial constitutional issues facing the new Dominion, the British North America Act of 1867 was carefully explicit in providing for the future admission of "Rupert's Land and the North-Western Territory" to Confederation. Of course there would be gigantic problems. Even removing the enfeebled grip of the current proprietors, the Hudson's Bay Company, would require negotiations and money. The deplorable state of Anglo-American relations as an aftermath of the Civil War gave added significance to the cries of American anglophobes and Minnesota expansionists for the annexation of the British North-West. Even when the region was acquired, there would be formidable problems of communication. The Palliser expedition had solemnly reported that the only natural route to the North-West was along the Red River and through the United States. True, the Canadian-sponsored Hind expedition had disagreed. Its surveyor, S. J. Dawson, claimed that a non-American route was possible, combining canoes and wagon trails. Whatever the route, it would be either difficult and expensive or politically embarassing—and possibly both.

Very low on the agenda of Canadians who pondered the problems of the North-West, sometimes even out of sight, was any consideration of the feelings of the people who already lived there. The negotiations with the Hudson's Bay Company and with the financiers and speculators who might link the territory to Canada with rail lines and telegraph wires were conducted over the heads of the ten thousand white and mixed blood settlers in the Red River valley and the twenty or thirty thousand Indians who lived farther west. Even the handful of Company servants who actually provided the vestigial civil administration of the territory were ignored. Only the Canadians, the arrogant and detested vanguard of the Ontarians who would eventually dominate Manitoba, seemed to be privy to the decisions about the future.

By the actions of one man, Canadian politicians and the titled magnates who controlled the affairs of the Hudson's Bay Company were compelled to pay attention to the feelings of the local people. Louis Riel was born in Saint Boniface in 1844, of almost purely French-Canadian descent but with just enough Indian blood to qualify as Métis—descendants of the voyageurs and trappers and traders who had come from the East, and their Indian wives. The Métis, halfbreeds, *bois brûlés,* had developed what was, in effect, their own civilization. Indifferent farmers, generous, a little improvident, they were also skilful and highly organized buffalo hunters. The disciplined structure they adopted for the hunt also helped make the Métis an impressive fighting force, as their epic victory over the Sioux at Grand Coteau in 1851 had demonstrated. Small wonder that Riel should grow up with a powerful sense of the special tradition and mission of his halfbreed people. He had been a boy of quick

The Red River cart was one of the artifacts of the Métis culture. Made from wood and buffalo hide, without metal, it illustrated the Métis ability to adapt to a difficult environment.

Louis Riel, from a photograph taken in 1884. His people saw him as the statesman who could deal effectively with Ottawa.

intelligence, sufficient for Bishop Taché of Saint Boniface to send him to Montreal to gain a classical education among the sons of some of the most influential French-Canadian families. It was a rare experience for a Métis to confront, first hand, the life and culture of the world at large and it probably strengthened Riel's growing conviction that he was a specially chosen individual among a specially ordained people. When he finally returned to the Red River colony in 1868, he was already determined to "busy himself with public affairs whenever the moment arose."

That moment soon arrived. After 1867, the transfer of the Red River colony to Canada seemed merely a matter of time. As the Métis contemplated this prospect, they shared many fears and some real grievances. The few Canadians who had reached the colony—domineering, contemptuous and commercially shrewd—were an alarming advertisement for those who might follow. When survey parties arrived from Canada in 1868, there were practical reasons for alarm. Technically, the Métis were only squatters on Hudson's Bay Company land. Moreover, their farms, running back from the river front in narrow strips, as in Quebec, did not fit into the grid pattern which the Ontario-born surveyors had inevitably brought to their latest assignment. Above all, there was a growing anger at the way the people of the Red River were being treated by Canada, the absence of consultation and the lack of representative institutions in the arrangements being made for the new government of the colony. The directors of the Hudson's Bay Company were content with a cash payment of £300,000 and generous land grants but Company representatives in the North-West felt as cheated and ignored as the ordinary settlers. The last governor of Assiniboia, William Mactavish, was a sick and dying man.

The result was the crisis of 1869-70. It was not created by Louis Riel. He did little or nothing to arouse the sense of grievance among the French or English halfbreeds but, once it existed, his eloquence in both languages gave it political form and his determination and leadership established the provisional government. By effectively filling the power vacuum which developed between the Company's surrender and the Canadian takeover, Riel was able to compel the Canadian government to negotiate directly with the spokesmen of the Red River settlers. The outcome, in the form of the Manitoba Act, gave the tiny colony the status of a province, secured recognition (illusory, as time would prove) for the equal rights of French and English, and won for the Métis full recognition of their claims to land.

By establishing his provisional government and by repelling William MacDougall, who arrived prematurely to assert his own authority and that of the Canadian government, Riel challenged both the Canadian party in the colony and the authority of both the British and the Canadian governments. In itself, that was not fatal. After a series of foolish

The murder of Thomas Scott at Fort Garry in 1870. Drawings like this one in the *Canadian Illustrated News* helped fuel passions against Riel and his followers, with tragic long-term consequences.

and ill-conceived attempts to overthrow Riel, the leaders of the Canadian party were locked up in Fort Garry, hostages in any future negotiations with Ottawa. Faced by the rebuff to MacDougall, the Canadian authorities simply handed the problem back to Great Britain and, after stiff bargaining, both governments agreed to send a joint military expedition to the Red River in the summer of 1870 to show the flag. However, circumstances changed. To demonstrate the authority of his provisional government to its faltering subjects, once and for all, Riel insisted upon a brutal and foolish act. Thomas Scott, a troublesome Ontario Orangeman among his captives, was put to death. For months, many in English Canada had chafed at the delays and compromises involved in acquiring the new territory. Protestant bigots had been furious that Catholic clergy at the Red River were wholeheartedly involved in Riel's challenge to Ottawa. The killing of Scott gave both groups a rallying cry which echoed and re-echoed across Ontario throughout 1870. Instead of being simply a military excursion to test the feasibility of Dawson's all-Canadian route to the Red River, the Red River expedition under Colonel Garnet Wolseley became, at least in the public mind, a mission to crush revolt and hang the murderers of Thomas Scott. Most of its members were sorely disappointed to discover, after their arduous trek, that Fort Garry was empty and the provisional government had vanished.

Time and the cool management of the first Canadian lieutenant-governor, A. G. Archibald, allowed bitterness in Manitoba to subside. Although he had fled at the approach of Wolseley's troops, Riel was convinced that he had deserved well of the Canadian government. He was, after all, the architect of Manitoba's provincial status and he had firmly resisted the pressures to link the colony with the United States. In 1871, when an abortive Fenian threat faced the province, Riel led other Métis in offering his support to the government. In 1873 and again in 1874, he was acclaimed M.P. for the federal constituency of Provencher.

The heat and indignation remained almost exclusively in eastern Canada. While French-Canadians could find little to criticize in the conduct of the Métis leader, it was different in Ontario. Toronto nationalists, speaking through "Canada First," had campaigned for Manitoba as an English-speaking, Protestant extension of Ontario since they had first found their voices. From the moment Colonel George Denison had received a piece of the rope which had allegedly bound Scott's hands, the fate of the murdered Orangeman was exploited on platforms across the province. When the Conservative government in Ottawa considered fulfilling its half-promise of an amnesty for Riel and his associates, the Ontario Liberals, under Edward Blake, carefully stoked the resulting indignation and won the provincial election of 1871.

The fury of Ontario against the murderer, Riel, fuelled by raw prejudice and political opportunism, soon drew a corresponding anger from French Canada. Both Sir John A. Macdonald, as leader of the Conservatives, and the Liberal leader, Alexander Mackenzie, found that the Riel issue divided their followers. At the start of the 1873 session of Parliament, French-Canadian Conservatives, led by L. F. R. Masson, a friend from Riel's school days, warned Macdonald that they would withdraw their support unless he proclaimed an amnesty. With characteristic adroitness, the Prime Minister evaded the issue and, by the time it arose again, it was his Liberal rival, Mackenzie, who was in power. Early in the 1874 session, escorted by Quebec M.Ps. and braving a warrant and a reward of $5,000 for his capture, Riel actually entered the Parliament Buildings and took his oath as M.P. A few days later, although he had not actually taken his seat, he was formally expelled in a vote which ignored party lines.

Riel was still free but Ambrose Lépine, the president of the Métis court which had condemned Scott, was less fortunate. He was arrested, tried and sentenced to hang. At last the issue had to be faced. Either an amnesty must be proclaimed or Lépine would die, releasing an explosion of racial antagonism. For the unfortunate Mackenzie, there was no escape from the dilemma his predecessor had sidestepped. Or was there? At the decisive moment, the Governor-General, Lord Dufferin, deliberately exercised the royal prerogative of mercy without asking the advice of his Canadian ministers. At one stroke, Dufferin saved Lépine, his ministers and the peace of Canada in return for scolding memoranda

Sir John A. Macdonald. Long years in politics had persuaded him that inaction was often as useful a response to problems as any. In the North-West at least, history would prove him wrong.

from Edward Blake, now the Liberal Minister of Justice, and the abrogation of a vice-regal prerogative which might have been equally convenient ten years later.

Louis Riel's first excursion into civil disobedience had illustrated two recurrent factors in Canadian policy for the North-West. The local people, however far off, however scorned by Ottawa officialdom, could not be ignored indefinitely. And, in dealing with them, the profound divisions between French- and English-Canadians might very easily be exposed. Fifteen years after the collapse of Riel's provisional government, the potency of both factors would again be illustrated.[3]

Many of the halfbreeds of the Red River colony, particularly those of English-speaking background, remained in the new province of Manitoba. Others, still resentful of their treatment, detesting the newcomers from the East, moved farther west, selling the land they had been granted under the Manitoba Act to speculators, often at a fraction of the value. The West meant the prairie, a limitless domain with a seemingly inexhaustible supply of buffalo. Already there were a few Métis settlements scattered along the prairie rivers but most of the Manitobans formed a new community at St. Laurent, on the banks of the South Saskatchewan. Remote from civilization and Canadian officialdom, the Métis even experimented with their own constitution, appointing Gabriel

Blackfoot Indians migrating. The approach of the white man sealed the fate of the traditional Indian way of life. The near-extermination of the buffalo was only the symptom.

Dumont their first "president". A detachment of the newly created North West Mounted Police was hurriedly despatched to investigate reports of a new "Red River Rebellion" and a surprised and embarrassed Dumont promptly laid down his office.

The Métis settlement at St. Laurent prospered. By the early 1880s, more halfbreed parishes had been established in the vicinity, among them, in 1881, St. Antoine de Padoue, better known as Batoche. However, the way of life that had attracted the Métis from Manitoba had ended. By the winter of 1879, the last of the great herds of buffalo had been slaughtered. The pattern of existence which both Indians and Métis had known since time out of mind suddenly became impossible. The only available alternative for both the indigenous peoples of the plains was the dreary, backbreaking work of farming. For the Métis, even that was uncertain. The Indians at least had reserves, secured in perpetuity by a series of treaties, while the white settlers, now pushing their way into the North-West, could obtain government land grants. Only the Métis were squatters. If they were long-established in the Territories, there was no provision to grant them land; if they had come from Manitoba, they had already forfeited their claim for a free grant. Even if the halfbreeds could persuade the government to listen to their plight, it was apparent that the long, thin riverfront lots which they had laid out for themselves would not fit the neat, systematic grid that government surveyors were laying out across the prairies. As in every other serious matter, the government was slow to move. Eventually it made allowances for the long-established Métis settlements like St. Albert, but there was no comfort for the people of St. Laurent. While the Department of the Interior opened a Land Office in the white community of Prince Albert, the government still ignored the Métis on the South Saskatchewan. Even when Ottawa sent an agent to investigate half-breed land claims around Prince Albert, the government's man spoke only English and did not even approach the French-speaking Métis.

The Métis were far from alone in their discontent. In the years after 1870, urged on by the great land hunger which swept all of North America, white settlers hurried to the North-West to find space for themselves and their families. Prince Albert, originally established by retired servants of the Hudson's Bay Company, soon became the largest white settlement in the Territories, a minor boom town on the North Saskatchewan. Farther up the river Battleford was a rival, particularly after 1877 when it was selected to be the territorial capital. However, the pioneers rapidly found that life on the frontier was lonely, grim and unrewarding. Prices for necessities were high, land regulations seemed bureaucratic and unrealistic and early frosts mocked the settlers' attempts to raise crops.

When the Macdonald government returned to office in 1878, its most ambitious undertaking was the completion of the railway to the Pacific. By 1880, a contract had been arranged and the Canadian North-West's greatest single problem—its physical isolation from the rest of the coun-

White settlers near Saskatoon. Dismayed by the hardships of the new land, misled by the promises which had led them there, many white settlers were as close to revolt in 1884 as the Métis.

try—seemed to be solved. The granting of the C.P.R. charter helped start a land boom which did much to reconcile settlers to the grim realities of their daily lives. It seemed certain that the railway line would avoid the arid desert of the Palliser Triangle, swinging north and west through settlements and communities like Prince Albert, Battleford and Edmonton, where the bulk of the people had taken up land. That was where average rainfalls offered the best guarantee of successful farming and that was where most of the speculators had sunk their money, certain of handsome returns. Instead, to their dismay, the C.P.R. line headed straight west from Winnipeg, across the dry land, hugging the American border to cut off any rival lines from the Northern Pacific. The land boom collapsed. This disaster coincided with the deliberate depression of western grain prices at Montreal and the beginning of a period of crop failure.

For the first but by no means the last time, the West found itself in the grip of widespread economic disaster. Farmers and businessmen alike found themselves facing ruin as a result of decisions far beyond their control. Immigration slowed to a trickle. Even with bad harvests, agricultural prices sagged. Work for teamsters, a standby occupation for whites and Métis alike, dwindled. Late in 1883, angry delegates met to form the Manitoba and North-West Farmers' Union and to send the first of many delegations to Ottawa. Like so many of their successors, the delegates returned angry and empty-handed. The only specific response of the government to the Farmers' Union was to authorize a new militia battalion for Winnipeg, the 90th Rifles. That accomplished, the government could perhaps afford to be philosophical about schoolhouse meetings and settlers' committees. The troublemakers, one government official assured his superiors, were all Liberals, "some of the most rabid kind". To Sir John A. Macdonald, the survivor of so many petitions and grievances, "no amount of concession will prevent . . . people from grumbling and agitating."[4]

There was at least some justice in the government's reaction. Some of the most active agitators were transplanted Liberals like the Jackson family of Prince Albert or Frank Oliver, the aggressive editor of the Edmonton *Bulletin*. "If history be taken as a guide," Oliver told his readers, "what could be plainer than that without rebellion the people of the West need expect nothing. While with rebellion, successful or otherwise, they may reasonably expect to get their rights."[5]

By 1884, such incitements were striking home. Unrepresented in Ottawa—and only by one man in the Territorial Council—whites and halfbreeds in the district of Lorne, which embraced both Prince Albert and the Métis settlements on the South Saskatchewan, remembered the man who, once before, had made a government listen. It was not a congenial decision. White settlers, chiefly from Ontario, had to overcome

In eastern Canada, it was tempting to share J. W. Bengough's belief that agitation in the North-West had been manufactured by the Liberals to embarrass the Macdonald government.

MERELY A HUM-BUG-BEAR!

their memories of Thomas Scott while English-speaking halfbreeds from Manitoba still felt that Riel had gone too far in 1870.

But Riel was a changed man. The intervening years had been tragically hard. For close to ten years, he had wandered the United States, a lonely, embittered exile, constantly recalling the persecution he had suffered, increasingly subject to religious fantasies. For twenty months he had been an inmate of insane asylums in Quebec and the experience had done nothing to restore his mental balance. By 1884 he was sustaining himself and his family as a poorly paid teacher at a mission station in Montana, only intermittently in touch with affairs in the North-West.

To the settlers of the district of Lorne, however, Riel's reputation remained undiminished. There was no one else of stature to reach across the gulf that separated the white and Métis communities. Even among the Métis, there was no other possible leader, not even the solid, sensible Gabriel Dumont and certainly not the former Manitoba cabinet minister, Charles Nolin, whom few really trusted. Financed with money raised by whites and halfbreeds alike, a little delegation set out for Montana to find Riel and bring him back to the Saskatchewan.

On June 4th, 1884, they found him at St. Peter's mission in Montana. It can have taken little persuasion by Gabriel Dumont and others in the group because, next day, Riel had agreed that he and his family would ride north with them, preparing for the ultimate mission of his life. By the end of June, the party had reached St. Laurent and a series of meetings had been planned which would take Riel through the district. On July 19th, nervous and uncertain, he was in Prince Albert, among English-Canadians who only fifteen years before had demanded that he be hanged. Now, modest and full of trepidation, he won them over with a "quiet and gentle way". In William Henry Jackson, Riel found an educated, articulate (if increasingly unbalanced) agent among the whites.[6] By the autumn of 1884, aided by crop failure and the inadequacy of the government's response to a series of letters, petitions, resolutions and warnings, Riel appeared to have consolidated his support among both Métis and white communities. It was a remarkable political achievement but it was counter-balanced by his relations with two other groups in his vast community, the priests and the Indians.

The Métis settlements had grown up around mission stations served by devout, unsophisticated priests of the Oblate order, men who had shared every hardship of their flock and who had won their love and respect. In 1869-70, Riel's links with the clergy had been close. In Father Ritchot he had had a relentless negotiator for the rights of the Métis while Bishop Taché, once he had returned from Rome, was the most powerful single influence on Riel. In 1884, it was different. In his fevered religious meditations, Riel had come to the conclusion that the Catholic Church had been undermined and betrayed by its traditional European leaders; that it was ordained by God that the Church be founded anew among the Métis people; and that its new pope must be Bishop Grandin of St. Albert. Such notions, and their elaborations, appalled the missionaries and their alarm grew when they discovered that their influence over the Métis was being supplanted by that of the newcomer. To the halfbreeds, Riel's mysticism, his long prayers, his self-denial were marks of a man even closer to God than their priests. From the first, Father André, the most patriarchal of the Oblates, had suspected Riel and had urged the government to remove him, by bribery if necessary. Gradually other priests, who had shared the community's hopes for Riel, joined his opponents.

Even more crucial for Riel's future course of action was his determination to make common cause with the Indians. By 1884 there were more than 26,000 of them in the Canadian North-West and their plight was tragic. The annihilation of the buffalo meant a choice between starvation or being cooped up on small reserves, condemned to a life of ploughing and sowing and government bacon. It was a miserable choice and it took five years of starvation and destitution until the last of the Indian bands, a group of irreconcilable Crees led by a little, ugly, proud-spirited man named Big Bear, could be forced to take up its reserve.[7] Once on the reserve, reactions to a repellent new way of life ranged from apathy to violent anger. Cattle, supplied by the government, were slaughtered

Indians watching a C.P.R. train. The arrival of the railway affected everyone in the west—and for many of them, whites, Indians and Metis alike, the impact seemed to be harmful.

for meat and seed corn was eaten. Farm instructors, employed to train the Indians for their new life, fell into despair and withdrew to till their own fields. To make matters worse, renewed hard times in Canada forced the Dominion government to try to trim costs. Lawrence Vankoughnet, the civil servant in charge of Indian administration, willingly played his part. Too much government help would make the Indians permanently dependent, he argued, and the economy drive became an excuse for cutting down rations, reducing staff and requiring that even trivial decisions should be made in Ottawa. The new policy meant, in practice, starvation. For the first time since the Mounted Police had come west, there were violent confrontations with angry Indians. At Crooked Lakes in February, 1884, a force of police was openly defied; that summer, at Poundmaker's reserve on the Battle River, there was almost a pitched battle between Superintendent Crozier's men and Crees assembled for a thirst dance.

However, when Riel's messengers moved out among the Indian bands, they received a mixed response. Some, particularly those who had been among the last to accept reserve life, welcomed almost any excuse to revolt. Others were plainly determined to wait until they could see how a challenge to the white man's authority would fare. And even the most angry were hesitant about making common cause with Riel. In the settlement of the West, the Métis had often been the indispensable intermediaries between the whites and the Indians but, in times of crisis, they had invariably turned to the white side of their heritage. Indians were not yet prepared to trust their fate unreservedly even to the dynamic new prophet at Batoche.

Edgar Dewdney, lieutenant governor of the North-West Territories. A sensible, kindly man, he found himself torn between the conflicting demands of people in the Territories and his masters in Ottawa.

Angry opposition from the missionaries, restrained receptions from the Indians: these were the counterbalances to Riel's apparent success in winning support from his own people and from many of the white settlers. Indeed, they were worse than counterbalances. Common cause among all three of the major groups on the prairies was out of the question. Desperate and angry the white settlers might be, but not to the extent of risking an Indian war. The Minnesota massacres of 1862 and the Sioux wars of the 1870s were lively and horrible memories. Simply by seeking support from Indians who had fared more tragically than any other group on the prairies, Riel forfeited the support of the whites and, with it, all serious hope of bringing effective political pressure to bear on the government in Ottawa.

As for the Métis, an alliance with the Indians was merely uncomfortable; the alienation of their priests mattered far more. Publicly, they cheered Riel, delighting in the thought that his vision of God rendered them a chosen people. Even privately, they could see their leader as a man of extraordinary faith and piety. Yet the opposition of their priests was troubling, a cause for reserving enthusiasm, for taking a few less chances. As among the Indians, there would be many who would watch and wait; only a few would commit themselves without reserve. When the extent of Riel's plan to defy the government became more explicit, all the more hung back. As in 1870, Riel struggled to assert his authority, uttering public threats against the priests, trying and sentencing Charles Nolin to death and then reprieving that timid and irresolute man only after he swore solemnly to keep the faith.

Gradually, perhaps a little too late, it was becoming apparent to the Métis that even with Riel amongst them, still as beloved and as influential as ever, times had changed since 1870. One difference was that Canadian authority was now firmly established in the North-West, not merely waiting at Pembina. At Regina, capital of the Territories since the C.P.R. line had been settled, sat Edgar Dewdney, Indian Commissioner for the Territories since 1879 and Lieutenant-Governor since 1881. He was an English-born engineer, a former Conservative M.P. from British Columbia, a big, kindly man and a faithful, if unimaginative, administrator, who suffered as much as anyone the agonies of dealing with the remote and unresponsive Ottawa government. Dewdney was fully informed of the discontent in his territory and, within the narrow limits allowed him by Ottawa officialdom, he struggled to bring relief, finding a few extra rations for starving Indians, seeking a few dollars for public works to employ destitute Métis at St. Laurent and opening vacancies for Indian agents and farm instructors to halfbreeds

The North-West Territories Council meeting in Regina. Partly appointed, partly elected, the council had little responsibility or prestige, even as a sounding board for local opinion.

Commissioner Acheson G. Irvine of the North-West Mounted Police. A former militia officer, Irvine had the confidence of his officers and men.

rather than to the political appointees who clamoured for them. Yet, like Macdonald, Dewdney tended to blame the agitator more than the grievances for the discontent among the Métis: "That ruffian Riel," he fumed, "can make them do anything."[8]

What Dewdney needed was time—time to persuade the Indians to accept their dreary future, time to harvest a few successful crops, time to settle the land problems of white settlers and Métis and time to deal with Riel and to persuade him, by threats or promises, to return to Montana. Perhaps with the coming of the spring of 1885 he would be able to journey north, to see for himself the ravages of the hard winter,

to meet Riel and his associates, to negotiate. And, so far as his Ottawa superiors were concerned, he could have all the time he needed. Sir John A. Macdonald (who retained the title of Superintendant-General of Indian Affairs) and his Minister of the Interior, David Macpherson, were now old men, inclined to let time solve all problems. The Métis were not so patient.

Dewdney's sole recourse against the threats of Métis insurrection and Indian uprising, telegraphed to him by panicky agents and settlers, was the North West Mounted Police. To patrol an area of a hundred thousand square miles, the force had been expanded to a strength of five hundred and fifty men. Two hundred of them, under the redoubtable Superintendent Crozier, were already concentrated in posts at Battleford, Carlton and Prince Albert. In the early months of 1885, as the warnings from the north grew more strident, the Commissioner, Lieutenant-Colonel A. G. Irvine, carefully scraped together reinforcements from the badly undermanned southern posts. On March 18th, with ninety men, he set off for Prince Albert.

Irvine's preparations were known to Riel and his followers. The winter had seen a sudden cooling in the relations between whites and Métis and the prospect of police reinforcements was now welcomed with delight at Prince Albert—not least because more men would mean more business for the town's merchants. To the Métis, however, it meant that the government had decided to crush their feeble protest with force. It had been a miserable winter for them and worse still for Riel. Penniless, he had been forced to seek charity from his followers. Perhaps Father André had been right. Desperate and downhearted, unable even to feed his family, Riel might have accepted a few thousand dollars from the government as the price of slipping back over the American border. But now it was too late. On the evening of March 18th, Riel's followers seized the local Indian agent and other government officials. A police inspector narrowly escaped. The next day was the feast of St. Joseph, patron saint of the Métis, a fitting occasion for Riel to announce his second provisional government and to appoint a council named, from his ill-remembered Latin, the Exovedate—"taken from the sheep". Establishing his headquarters at Batoche, Riel despatched couriers to rally the other halfbreed settlements and the Indian reserves. Confused and expectant, the North West waited while both Riel and the police assembled their forces.

Irvine's column, moving with impressive speed despite bitter winter conditions, covered the three hundred miles from Regina in less than a week. On March 24th the police reached Prince Albert. Assured that all was quiet, Irvine gave his men and horses a day to rest before pushing forward on the final stage to Fort Carlton. It was a fatal delay. Irvine was almost in sight of Carlton on the afternoon of the 26th when he

The murders at Frog Lake. Though whites were quick to attribute the cruel events at Frog Lake to Big Bear, the Cree chief was away when they were planned and did his best to stop the massacre.

learned of the disastrous encounter at Duck Lake. That evening he reached a painful decision. Carlton would have to be abandoned. As a fort, it was utterly indefensible, a mere cluster of wooden buildings, vulnerable at every point to an enemy stationed on the bank behind. The special constables from Prince Albert, moreover, were now desperate to return to their defenceless wives and children. In the darkness, sleighs were loaded and surplus supplies were sunk under the ice of the river. Suddenly, straw near an overheated stove caught fire. Within minutes, the decrepit old buildings were engulfed in an inferno. The wounded from Duck Lake were hastily dragged outside and loaded on the sleighs. As flames lit the sky, the column began to move. By dawn Carlton was in ruins and the police were in full retreat along the trail to Prince Albert.

News of the defeat of the police spread rapidly. Indians and Métis grew more confident while terror seized the little prairie communities and isolated homesteads of the white settlers. Some of them a year before had begun organizing home guards and appealing to the government for arms and ammunition; now their demands approached frenzy. Others abandoned all that they owned to flee to Prince Albert or Battleford. Across the Territories there were a few scattered murders as Indians paid off old scores. Mission stations and Hudson's Bay Company stores were pillaged.

The worst tragedy occurred at Frog Lake, near the reserve which Big Bear had so reluctantly accepted. The local Indian agent, Thomas Quinn, was a halfbreed, confident that he could command the respect of his charges. To ensure peace he sent away the tiny local police detachment. Quinn's confidence was misplaced. On April 2nd, a week after Duck Lake, the Indians struck. Big Bear was away hunting, and the initiative came from even more recalcitrant members of the band, Imasees and Wandering Spirit. The whites and halfbreeds at Frog Lake were seized; by the end of the day, nine of them, including Quinn and two Roman Catholic priests, were dead. Of the whites, only the Hudson's Bay Company agent and the widows of two of the murdered men survived.[9]

After a few days of pillaging and destruction the Indians moved on to Fort Pitt, a Hudson's Bay post which twenty-five police desperately struggled to bring to a state of defence. It was a grim prospect. Like Carlton, Pitt was a total misnomer for a fort. The wooden buildings were obviously vulnerable to fire and the only water supply was outside the walls. The fort sheltered many civilians too, and their leader, W. J. McLean, chief agent for the Hudson's Bay Company, weighed their fate. A man of many years experience with the Indians, McLean concluded that it would be safer for his people to surrender to Big Bear than to share in a hopeless defence. Accordingly, the civilians left the fort to give themselves up. For Inspector Francis Dickens, a son of the famous novelist, who commanded the little police detachment, McLean's decision to trust the safety of white men, women and children to the Indians was a mortal personal humiliation. However, McLean had also relieved him and his men of their last reason for staying. That night, the police embarked in a leaky scow to make their perilous way down the North Saskatchewan river to Battleford.

The fall of Fort Pitt on April 15th climaxed a period of unbroken triumph for both Métis and Indians. In a series of devastating blows, Canadian authority in the North-West had been badly undermined. The police had been chased from the field at Duck Lake, leaving their dead on the ground; forts at Carlton and Pitt had been given up without a fight; white property had been pillaged without opposition. At Battleford, terrified settlers watched helplessly from the walls of the police fort as their homes were ransacked and burned.

At the same time, the rebellion had reached its full extent. While panicky settlements from the Rockies to Port Arthur on Lake Superior appealed for protection, the limitations of Riel's grand design were fast becoming apparent. Far from arousing a great native insurrection, barely a thousand Indians had responded to his appeal; indeed, the two most prominent rebel chiefs, Big Bear at Fort Pitt and Poundmaker at Battleford, were being pushed as far as they were by younger, more aggressive men. Even more serious for Riel, other Indians showed no sign of moving to his support. They stayed where they were—near Fort Pitt and at Cut Knife Hill, west of Battleford. Only Indians from nearby reserves, like the Teton Sioux, came to Batoche. Even the Métis were far from united. At most, Riel and Dumont could count on three to four hundred fighting men, and few of them were really well-armed.

Among western settlers and eastern Canadians alike, the military potential of the Métis and Indians was greatly over-estimated. "The modern brave . . ." Lord Lansdowne informed the Colonial Secretary, "thinks more of tobacco and pork than of human scalps,"[10] but privately the Governor-General was as apprehensive as anyone about the dangers the country now faced. The memory of the American military disaster at the Little Big Horn, where highly-trained cavalry had been slaughtered by Sitting Bull's Sioux only nine years before, exercised a powerful influence on Canadian opinion, sustaining a popular image of the Métis and Indians as well-armed, eagle-eyed marksmen superbly mounted. It was a fair description of some of them, like Gabriel Dumont and his brothers, or the war chiefs of the Crees and Assiniboines; but they were a minority. Most Indians and Métis were fortunate to have a single, worn-out shotgun. Ammunition was in desperately short supply. Although the police had been defeated, they had yet to surrender any significant quantity of arms or ammunition.

Furthermore, both Indians and Métis fought essentially as individuals, following orders only by inclination. The intense internal democracy of the Indian tribe was a weak basis for planning military strategy; it encouraged the inertia which was to allow the inexperienced, baggage-laden Canadian militia to win the initiative. While he gave his people brilliant inspiration, as a war leader Riel was hopelessly irresolute, impeding his shrewd and experienced lieutenant, Gabriel Dumont, at every turn.

To Canadians, however, these weaknesses were as yet unknown. While heedless crowds in the eastern cities chattered about the new excitement, Thomas White, editor of the Conservative Montreal *Gazette,* gloomily wrote to Sir Charles Tupper, Canadian High Commissioner in London: "Things are in a terrible condition in the North-West, and it is difficult to overestimate the damage that will result. It is such a vast country that it is impossible to see where the trouble may end. Of course it will be put down, but the cost in life and treasure will be very great."[11]

II. The Government Reacts

The day after Irvine left Regina to march north, Dewdney himself left for Winnipeg. The news from the North seemed better and, once Irvine's reinforcements were in position, it would be time for Dewdney to join him, to open negotiations with Riel in person. Meanwhile, arrangements had to be made in Winnipeg to purchase seed grain for the coming season and Dewdney also wanted to arrange possible military reinforcements for his desperately overstretched police force. Trouble, he still believed, could be averted if only he were given time. There was also the embarrassing matter of the terms he could offer Riel. If the missionaries were right, how much would it cost to persuade Riel to abandon his people? "My name is Riel and I want Material" he had joked to D. H. McDowall, Lorne's representative on the Territorial Council, who had conveyed the information to the lieutenant governor. "Government should go as far as justice will permit in giving me full discretion to act," Dewdney now wired Macdonald from Winnipeg. "In the event of mission failing, must have a large force at command who are sufficiently strong at first blow to overcome the half breed and Indian population."[1]

In fact the Prime Minister had sent his orders the day before. "We are not aware of any causes for discontent," he wired. The land claims of the Métis would be adjusted as soon as a commission could collect evidence but the government's intention was to "enforce the law and keep the peace".[2] Instead of a basis for bargaining Dewdney would be given militia.

Dominion military resources in the North-West and in the adjoining province of Manitoba were feeble. Until 1877, a small permanent garrison had been maintained in Winnipeg—a remnant of the Red River expedition of 1870. Then, as an economy measure, it had been disbanded, its arms, equipment and clothing left to rot and rust in the half-abandoned buildings of Fort Osborne. Although many settlers in the

Lieutenant Colonel Charles F. Houghton, Deputy Adjutant General for Military District No. 10: "not much head and still less judgement."

west had had a smattering of training in the volunteer militia, the only organized militia units between the Great Lakes and the Rockies were in Winnipeg, a city of only 8,000 people. In addition to the 90th Rifles, hastily authorized little more than a year before, there was a small battery of field artillery and a little troop of cavalry. Manitoba and the North-West Territories formed Military District No. 10, under the command of Lieutenant-Colonel Charles F. Houghton, a forty-seven year old former British Army officer who, like Dewdney, had briefly entered politics as a Conservative M.P. from British Columbia. Houghton had served for fourteen years on the militia staff in British Columbia and Manitoba. When Hugh John Macdonald, the Prime Minister's son and a rising Winnipeg lawyer, had been asked for a private assessment of Houghton's ability, his report was not entirely reassuring. The staff officer was described as having "not much head and still less judgement." If he did not, as rumoured, go on "sprees" it was evident to the younger Macdonald, no abstainer himself, that "day in and day out he drinks more than is good for him."[3]

On March 22nd, now armed with authority to call on the Winnipeg militia, Dewdney telegraphed Macdonald: "Situation looks serious—think it imperative some able military man be on staff in the event of militia going north."[4] Well aware of Houghton's limitations, the Prime Minister immediately issued orders that Major-General Frederick Dobson Middleton, commanding the Canadian militia, should set out for the West. Middleton had only come to Canada in July, 1884. A short, stout, red-faced British infantry officer of fifty-nine, he was a veteran of hard fighting in New Zealand and India, and during the Indian Mutiny, he had twice been recommended for the Victoria Cross. He was also a soldier of some professional standing, a graduate of the staff college and formerly the commandant of the Royal Military College at Sandhurst. While serving in Canada years before, he had married a Montreal girl, Miss Eugénie Doucet. Much later, as he approached the age for compulsory retirement from the British Army, Middleton had used his Ca-

Major General Frederick Dobson Middleton. Perhaps not "the very model of a modern major general," but a shrewd and experienced soldier with a better awareness than his subordinates of the dangers of their undertaking.

nadian contacts to help get command of the militia, an appointment which carried the local rank of major-general. His predecessor, Major-General R. G. A. Luard, had been an abrasive, bad-tempered reformer. Middleton, anxious to hold his appointment for as long as he could, had quickly made up his mind to secure the favour of his political superiors by a careful mixture of flattery and compliance.

The General had little idea of the actual situation in the North-West. "I am inclined to think that there must be something serious or Sir John would not have consented to my being sent up,"[5] he commented in a hasty note to Lord Melgund, the Governor General's military secretary. Before he left Ottawa, Middleton had barely time to arrange for reinforcements to be sent from the East and to urge the government to buy two or three of the new American Gatling machine guns. Then he was off, travelling by rail through the United States. Early on March 27th he reached Winnipeg, only hours after the news of Duck Lake had arrived.

While Middleton was travelling, Colonel Houghton had been struggling with the problems of organizing the Winnipeg militia for active service. Jostled from his peacetime routine, the unfortunate staff officer had to obtain equipment, buy horses and arrange for supplies, all under the pressure of impatient directives from Ottawa and from Dewdney himself. Militiamen were reluctant to volunteer for service of unknown purpose and duration. The merchants, clerks and shop assistants who filled the ranks of the 90th Rifles knew that they were risking their jobs more certainly than their lives and, of the first hundred called, barely forty appeared. Until the 26th, of course, not even Dewdney expected a clash. "If report sent of collision & Police killed," he wired Macdonald on March 25th, "believe it incorrect. I have no advice of it."[6]

Duck Lake changed everything. By the evening of the 26th, Colonel Houghton and a full company of the 90th had set out on a C.P.R. special train for Troy, leaving the rest of the troops to get organized as best they could. Middleton arrived next morning to find Winnipeg in panic-stricken confusion. Pausing only to relay the latest information and to call for troops from the East, he took the rest of the 90th Rifles with him along the C.P.R. line to Qu'Appelle, the nearest point on the railway line to Batoche. By Saturday, the field battery from Winnipeg had joined him.

Further support would depend on the resources of the Canadian Militia in the East. An experienced military observer would have found it hard to believe that the Canadian military organization could cope with the kind of campaign now developing on the prairies. When the Dominion's first Militia Act was passed in 1868, the real defence of Canada depended on a substantial garrison of British regulars. The Canadian Militia was no more than an auxiliary for that garrison, a collec-

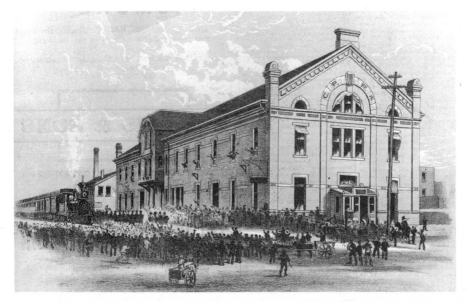

The 90th Winnipeg Rifles leaving for the 1885 campaign. Houghton's first attempt to call out troops was a failure but the news of Duck Lake brought a dramatic change of mood throughout the country.

tion of half-trained cavalry, artillery and infantry to swell the British ranks in the event of war or emergency. The British government provided cannon, obsolete leather accoutrements and Snider-Enfield rifles. British regulars trained the force and, in the event of active service, expected to provide it with a staff and to organize its transport and medical services. In 1870, when the Dominion had participated in the expedition to the Red River, a British officer had commanded the force and crack British regulars provided more than a third of the troops. The local British commander had also taken direct responsibility for managing the expedition, somewhat to the annoyance of the Canadian Department of Militia and Defence.

But in that same year, the British forces had begun to leave Canada. By the end of 1871, only a small garrison remained at Halifax. Deliberately, the Canadian government refused to replace the British in their military role. Only at the last possible moment were two small batteries of artillery created to take over abandoned British fortifications at Quebec and Kingston. These two units could at least provide training and an example to the militia artillery. Without the example of regulars, the militia infantry and cavalry simply stagnated. In the 1870's, declining government revenue accelerated the decay. In a country which faced no obvious military threat, the Militia department was an obvious target for economy. Since the political influence of militia officers prevented any major reduction in the size of the organization, the easiest economy was to cut down the number of rank and file and to reduce the amount of training to a mere twelve days a year. Even this much training was limited to the artillery and to battalions located in cities. The rural militia was assembled in makeshift summer camps only every other year.

This distinction split the Canadian force into two categories. Soon, the rural battalions consisted of little more than officers, with the bulk of the men recruited for each camp. In the cities, militia units could at least have a continuous existence, even if their training was usually limited to parades and displays of drill. In both the country and the cities, a militia commission was a badge of social and political distinction and, in major centres, it was an honour worth paying for. In a smart city corps, an officer not only purchased expensive uniforms and handed over his pay to the regimental fund; he could also be expected to make a handsome financial contribution. With this money, the city battalions developed into popular and prosperous social and athletic clubs. The Queen's Own Rifles of Toronto was perhaps the most impressive example. Uniforms and accessories were purchased in England and the regimental fund paid for equipment for the regimental pioneers and an ambulance section. While the Queen's Own Rifles took its military duties more seriously than some of the city battalions, it also sponsored a variety of sporting and social activities for its members and could even boast a well-drilled detachment for local theatrical performances.

Such private efforts could keep a military institution alive; they did not guarantee that it would work well. Recognizing this, the Canadian

Permanent force artillerymen practice rafting a gun. Canada's only full-time soldiers were the 750 men of the permanent corps, scattered in tiny schools of instruction.

Colonel Walker Powell, Adjutant General of the Canadian Militia. The senior Canadian-born staff officer had presided for twenty years over the peacetime administration of the force.

government slowly filled some of the gaps left by the British military withdrawal. In 1875, the practice of appointing a British colonel to act as Major General Commanding the Militia was incorporated in the Militia Act. In 1876, a military college was opened at Kingston. Arrangements were made in 1879 to manufacture ammunition for the now-obsolete Snider rifles at a new government-run cartridge factory at Quebec. Amendments to the Militia Act in 1883 allowed expansion of the two original artillery batteries into a permanent force of 750 men, permitting the addition of three small infantry companies and a troop of cavalry, each to serve as a school for its arm.

In its fundamentals, however, the Canadian militia of 1885 remained the military auxiliary of 1868. Militia Headquarters in Ottawa contained only four military officers: the General and his aide-de-camp; the Adjutant General (the senior Canadian-born officer in the force and a man who had been performing the same monotonous duties since 1862), and a retired British officer who served as inspector of artillery. A former militia officer and Liberal senator, Lieutenant-Colonel Charles Panet, presided as Deputy Minister over virtually every administrative responsibility in the Department. His staff of storekeepers and paymasters, despite their military ranks and titles, was civilian. Members usually owed their appointments to political influence. The Canadian militia,

Adolphe Caron, Minister of Militia and Defence. As the man responsible for organizing the campaign, he proved surprisingly energetic and decisive. Less surprisingly, he did not forget the rules of political patronage.

a later general officer commanding would claim, was "a collection of military units, without cohesion, without staff and without those departments by which an army is moved, fed or ministered to in sickness."[7]

The Hon. Adolphe Caron, Minister of Militia and Defence and M.P. for Quebec County, presided over this rag-tag military machine, In 1885, Adolphe Caron was forty-two, still the youngest member of the Cabinet and a fluently bilingual lawyer from Quebec city. Through his father, a former lieutenant-governor of Quebec, he served as a representative in Macdonald's government of the most conservative and clerical elements in his province. Unlike some of his predecessors, Caron had no personal military experience but he had many friends and political allies in the force. Since much of the Dominion's small military establishment was located at Quebec, Caron's portfolio gave him generous scope for political patronage in his own bailiwick. Like other contemporary cabinet ministers, Caron expected to make the final decision on even the most routine and trivial matters, a responsibility not even crisis could remove. In exercising his ministerial discretion, Caron paid close attention to the needs of his own party and political career although, to be fair, he was not incapable of stretching a point for a political opponent as well. Within Macdonald's government, the Minister of Militia was an obvious lightweight, overshadowed by more experienced and eminent French-Canadian colleagues like J. A. Chapleau or Sir Hector Langevin. The campaign in the North-West was virtually his first taste of serious responsibility in more than four years in office.

For the sake of immigration and railway investors, the Canadian government tried hard to minimise reports of trouble in the North-West. One Conservative newspaper dismissed Riel's seizure of prisoners on March 18th as "of no more consequence than a petty riot in any well settled part of old Canada".[8] However, in the following week, the federal government took some quiet precautions. The two permanent artillery batteries were ordered to prepare special detachments for active service. On his way through Toronto, Middleton notified Lieutenant-Colonel William Otter, the highly efficient commander of the local infantry school, that he and his men would be sent for if trouble occurred. On March 24th, Caron wired Harry Abbott, the C.P.R. superintendent of construction at Biscotasing, to make arrangements to send 400 men through to Winnipeg. That would be no easy matter. Winter still held a tight grip on Northern Ontario and the railway line was incomplete. Between Dog Lake and Nipigon, four gaps, totalling close to a hundred miles in length, broke the line. To help ferry the troops and their equipment from one stretch of rail to the next, horses and teams would be needed. Peremptory orders flowed along the telegraph wires.

Late on Friday evening, March 27th, the news from Duck Lake spread through Eastern Canada. In the House of Commons, Macdonald

Lieutenant Colonel William Otter and men of his infantry school. Though Toronto volunteers were eager to fight Riel, Otter had to depend on private charity to get them properly equipped for the campaign.

himself rose to confirm the rumours. From Winnipeg, Middleton wired: "Matter getting serious, better send all Regulars and good City Regiments. Experts say ought to have at least 2,000."[9] By the end of the evening, Caron could tell his general that 780 men were on the move. Telegrams from Militia Headquarters set both permanent batteries in motion. In Toronto, Otter's infantry school, the Queen's Own Rifles and the 10th Royal Grenadiers were mobilized. Thanks to prior notice, the gunners from Kingston and Quebec could board their trains on Saturday morning, heading for a rendezvous at Carleton Place. The Toronto contingent moved more slowly. Excited members of the two battalions had jammed the drill hall by dawn on Saturday but Otter found that most of the militiamen were ill-equipped for the rigours of winter soldiering. Though the train was waiting at the station, Otter delayed his departure until Monday morning while Toronto ladies and members of the city council scurried about, collecting underclothing, boots, mufflers and other comforts for the troops. This delay was in contrast to the permanent troops at Kingston who had left so rapidly that no arrangements had been made for the maintenance of their wives and children. The mayor reported that he was raising funds by subscription to keep them from want.

In Ottawa, would-be volunteers, contractors and job-seekers besieged the Minister's office. Captain A. Hamlyn Todd, son of the parliamentary librarian and an officer in the Governor General's Foot Guards, recalled later how a friendly M.P. elbowed him through the crowd to find Caron seated at a table with another cabinet minister and Colonel Panet, attempting to do business. Todd's project was to recruit sharpshooters from the local militia as a counterweight to the crack marksmen reportedly on the other side. Caron promptly approved and, by Tuesday, Todd and fifty Ottawa men were on their way. John Stewart, a Calgary rancher and former militia officer, happened to be visiting his brother, the Mayor of Ottawa. Caron sent him west to form a troop of scouts. Others received orders by telegram. Major General Thomas Bland Strange, a fire-eating former Royal Artillery Officer and commander of the permanent battery at Quebec, had retired to Calgary to try to make a success of his Military Colonization Ranch. "Would like to see you to the front again," Caron wired, "Trust to you as ever."[10]

So far, a predominantly English-speaking force had been thrown together by the Minister. Since the conflict with the largely French-speaking Métis would have sharp racial overtones, it was essential to consider

Toronto volunteers are mustered in the armouries. In summoning militia from Toronto, Caron was aware that they were probably among the most efficient in the Dominion. They were also likely to have long memories of Thomas Scott.

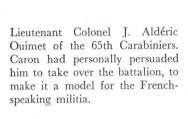

Lieutenant Colonel J. Aldéric Ouimet of the 65th Carabiniers. Caron had personally persuaded him to take over the battalion, to make it a model for the French-speaking militia.

the racial balance of the troops sent west. There were, it was true, many French Canadians in both of the permanent batteries; their attitude was that of military professionals anywhere at the prospect of combat. Their feeling was shared by young Oscar Pelletier, a militia subaltern from Quebec who was attending the military school at Kingston. He watched with growing envy as the troops prepared to depart but, since his father was a Liberal senator, he was, he later recalled, "in a very bad position to obtain favours in an orchestra in which politics played the first violin." With commendable initiative, Pelletier remembered a Conservative uncle who happened to be on excellent terms with Caron. With only three hours to spare, he won permission to accompany the Kingston battery.

Such spirit was hardly enough to achieve a proper representation for French Canada. Instead, Caron turned to the only two French-speaking city battalions, the 9th Voltigeurs of Quebec and the 65th Carabiniers Mont-Royal from Montreal. Both battalions were at a low ebb of efficiency but both commanding officers, Lieutenant Colonel Guillaume Amyot of the 9th and J. Aldéric Ouimet of the 65th were not only military enthusiasts but also Conservative M.P.s, eager to back up the government's policy. Of course, there were complications in sending French Canadians to fight Riel. Georges Beauregard, a private in the 9th, recalled being warned by passers-by in Quebec that he and his comrades would only be fighting French-speaking people like themselves and that they would be massacred for their pains. Dr. Emmanuel La-Chapelle, surgeon of the 65th, wrote to remind Caron that both he and Judge C. Aimé Dugas, a major in the battalion, had been schoolmates with the Métis leader and it would be better if the 65th were not sent at all: "you will doubtless not be unaware that several of our leading officers were close friends and college contemporaries of Louis Riel or that all our men regard the Métis as their compatriots and are not far from believing that the Métis demands have been made in our national interest and are no less just than those of our ancestors in 1837."[11]

In the event, LaChapelle and the deputy surgeon of the 65th stayed home, although Major Dugas and most of the other officers accepted the call to service. For second in command, Ouimet turned to Lieutenant Colonel Georges-A. Hughes, a veteran of the Papal Zouaves and a highly competent militia officer. It was more difficult to fill the ranks. Many of his own men were refused leave to serve by their civil employers and the gaps had to be filled by recruits from the street. One of them, Charles Daoust, later wrote a lengthy account of the battalion's services in the North-West; another, R. H. Metcalfe, later claimed that a tenth of the men in the ranks were English-speaking. A Montreal businessman wrote directly to Caron to explain that his bookkeeper, suspected of embezzlement, had enlisted to escape arrest. "I understand that had he undergone a Medical Examination he could not possibly have passed as he has had disease on him for a very long time."[12]

In Quebec, Colonel Amyot had similar difficulties in filling his battalion. Two companies of the 9th were formed by students from Laval University and the Rector was appalled at the hazards which his young charges would face, to say nothing of the disruption of the academic term. Others were equally alarmed: "To send children like these is causing real grief in the town," warned an anonymous correspondent, "The poor mothers are in despair and curses are raining on those who are taking their children from them."[13] When Caron promptly excused all the young soldiers of the 9th from service, the ranks of the battalion were very thin. Amyot left Quebec with 28 officers and only 204 other ranks. One company had only thirteen privates, another only eight.

However, as Robert Rumilly notes in describing the period: "The key fact to underline is that no one refused the province's share, no one at first took Riel's side."[14] Ten thousand people thronged the streets of Montreal to cheer the departing 65th and at Quebec a corresponding crowd, led by torch-bearing snowshoers accompanied the 9th to the station. Whatever grumbling and reservations there might be beneath the surface, Canada met her first great crisis as a united country.

Moreover, if there was reluctance to serve, it was by no means limited to French Canadians. Caron's own law partner, a major in the English-speaking 8th Rifles of Quebec, asked that he not be put in the embarrassing position of publicly having to refuse to serve. The colonel of a Montreal English-speaking battalion made a similar request, suggesting that only a few men from each of the local units be sent "without friction and without causing inconvenience."[15] Civilian employers firmly reminded the government that their special interests must not be forgotten in any sudden rush of patriotic enthusiasm.

As the first contingents headed west, orders reached more militia units. At Kingston, companies from seven rural militia battalions from counties east of Toronto were organized into the Midland Battalion, under Lieutenant Colonel Arthur Williams, the popular Conservative M.P. for East Durham. Another composite battalion was formed at Toronto from the York and Simcoe county battalions. Lieutenant Colonel W. E. O'Brien took command while Lieutenant Colonel Richard Tyrwhitt became the senior major. Both were Conservative M.P.s. At London, the 7th Fusiliers were called out. In Toronto, the widely known cavalry officer and activist in the earlier Riel affair, Lieutenant Colonel George T. Denison, took a different tack. He refused to offer his corps for service, he claimed, because as an inveterate critic of all politicians, the mere announcement that he wanted to go would be sufficient for the government not to send him. More than a week passed before Denison's cavalry troop, the Governor General's Body Guard, as well as the permanent force cavalry troop at Quebec, received their orders.[16]

Besides sending troops, Caron had somehow to furnish the force in the North-West with a staff and services. Lord Lansdowne's military secretary, Lord Melgund, was a former Guards officer who had used family connections and his rank in the Yeomanry to participate in British campaigns in India and Egypt. At the first news of trouble, he set off for the scene of action. Lieutenant-Colonel William Hayes Jackson, the militia staff officer at London, received orders to proceed directly to Winnipeg through the United States, to take charge of administration. Other officers and civilian officials of the department accompanied individual militia contingents along the C.P.R. route. The Minister borrowed telegraphers from the Dominion Government Telegraph Service and from the Great North-Western Telegraph Company to provide communications with the forces in the field.

The most difficult organization to improvise was medical care and military hospitals for the sick and wounded. While each militia unit included one or more surgeons, they were responsible only for the men in their own corps. The militia organization included no field hospitals, ambulances or even means of supplying bandages and medicine. Caron turned first to Dr. C. M. Douglas, a former surgeon in the British Army who had won the Victoria Cross for gallantry many years before. Douglas, a Canadian, had retired to Lakefield, north of Peterborough. After a few days of wrestling with the problem, the doctor confessed despair. "Suggest applying to U.S. Medical Department for help on ground common humanity,"[17] he wired the Minister. Instead, Caron turned to yet another Conservative M.P., Dr. Darby Bergin, who also happened to be commanding officer of the 59th Stormont Battalion. Newly appointed

Gilbert John Elliot, Lord Melgund, military secretary to Lord Lansdowne. A former officer in the Scots Guards, Melgund had served with the Turks in 1877, in Afghanistan in 1879 and in Egypt in 1882.

as surgeon general, the Cornwall doctor set to work with a fresh vigour. He named Senator Michael Sullivan, a Conservative doctor from Kingston, Purveyor General, to arrange for medical supplies and comforts for the sick and wounded. Dr. Thomas Roddick, a brilliant, athletic, 39 year-old surgeon from McGill University, was given command of a hastily organized field hospital, with the added responsibility of supervising all medical arrangements for the campaign. Another field hospital, commanded by Dr. Henri Casgrain of Windsor, soon followed. Rank and file for the two hospitals came from medical students at McGill and the University of Toronto. By April 12th, an amazingly short time, Roddick

Troops en route to the North-West. The first stage to Dog Lake was the easiest and few of the men in the cramped coaches realized the ordeal which awaited them.

and his hospital had reached Winnipeg, travelling through the United States. A few days later, the unit reached the newly established base at Swift Current.

While staff officers and medical men could travel through the United States, the government never seems to have considered any alternative to moving the bulk of its forces along the unfinished Canadian Pacific Railway route. Predictably, the Opposition leader, Edward Blake, accused the government of concealing the difficulties of the route around Lake Superior and urged the speed and common sense of applying to the American government for permission to travel through the United States. He was echoed by officials of the C.P.R.'s rival, the Grand Trunk. Indeed, there was every likelihood that the American authorities would have readily granted permission. In 1870 American border officials had done everything in their power to obstruct the Red River expedition but, in 1885 they showed every sign of co-operation. Rumours of Fenian movements and of arms shipments to the rebels dissipated as American troops moved up to patrol the international border. The Canadians and their baggage—including two carloads of ammunition—passed along

Men of the 10th Royal Grenadiers in open cars. On the stretches of rail, the troops were loaded on flatcars, roughly protected with board sides.

the American rail lines without difficulty. If the government preferred to use the C.P.R., it was less for fear of an American embargo than because it seemed to be there to be used. Probably Macdonald and Caron had little idea of how arduous the all-Canadian route would prove to be.

Virtually all the three thousand eastern militiamen who came west over the uncompleted line found that week of travel the most harrowing experience of the entire campaign. For men who, only a few days before, had been office clerks, shop assistants and factory hands, it was a rough introduction to the hardships of soldiering. Packed in open railway cars, they endured temperatures that sometimes went far below zero. Snow alternated with driving rain. Food, when it was available, consisted of salt pork, biscuit, rancid butter and unsweetened tea. Day after day, the troops were hungry, sleepless and wet. George Beauregard, moving with the 9th Voltigeurs, recalled the misery of being packed onto railway flatcars, sheltered only by a scrap of canvas: "There were fifty of us to a car, piled one on top of the other, drenched by the rain which fell on our backs in torrents. For the first time, we really knew what misery was. Without any way of warming ourselves, we could scarcely find the courage to revive our spirits by singing."[18]

Arthur Potvin, a young Laval medical student in the same battalion, later remembered that the bitter cold drove him to thoughts of suicide. One unfortunate man in the 65th did try to kill himself by diving under a railway car; he escaped with a crushed foot. A soldier in the 10th Royals went insane, threw off his clothes and attempted to leap on a bonfire. Not everyone suffered equally; on the longer stretches of track

Men who had been clerks, mechanics and shop assistants only a few days before, found themselves struggling with hardships which would have tested veteran troops.

The ordeal was even greater for the men and horses of the two artillery batteries. Knowing the difficulties, Van Horne had even suggested that they should be sent through the United States.

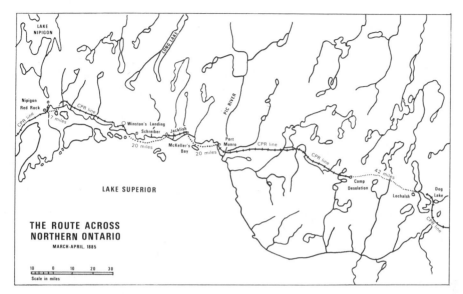

the makeshift trains included a caboose, usually commandeered by the officers.

The earlier contingents followed much the same route. Joining the C.P.R. line at Montreal or Carleton Place, the troops could travel in relative comfort to the end of rail at Lochalsh, near Dog Lake. There, Harry Abbott had marshalled a fleet of teams and sleighs to carry the troops and their equipment across a forty-two mile gap to a spot the soldiers soon christened Camp Desolation. Another stretch of railway ran ninety-two miles to Port Munro on Lake Superior. The troops were tightly jammed on flatcars, crudely walled around with canvas or boards, but almost completely exposed to snow and rain. At Port Munro, some of the men could find shelter in an old schooner, frozen in for the winter; others huddled in tents or around open fires. Next came a seventeen-mile march across the ice of Lake Superior to McKellar, a bitterly cold experience with the added misery of sunburn and frostbite. Colonel Otter had provided his men with goggles against the glare but, in spite of the precaution, he and many of his men were painfully snow-blinded by the end of the trek. The benumbed and worn out soldiers then boarded more flatcars for a fifteen-mile run to Jackfish Bay and a relatively straightforward march of fifteen miles to Winston's Landing. Another freezing fifty miles on flatcars brought them to Nipigon and a last, short stretch across the lake to Red Rock. However, for men already at the limits of exhaustion, those last few miles through the slush which covered the lake seemed interminable. It took the 10th Royals more than five hours to struggle across the lake and to climb into the roughly-built colonist cars which carried them straight through to Winnipeg.

For some, the journey was even harder. The gunners in the permanent force batteries had to find the extra strength to manhandle their guns and limbers on and off the flatcars and over the impossible places on the trail. Horses suffered even more than the men because they were denied even the meagre protection of the flatcar screens. William Van Horne, general manager of the C.P.R., had at first recommended that the horses and guns be shipped through the United States but Caron overruled him. The entire force would travel the C.P.R. route and it would go as fast as humanly possible. "Wish you to travel night and day," Caron wired the officers commanding the leading contingents, "I want to show what the Canadian Militia can do."[19] There was good reason for haste. Despite the bitterly cold weather of Northern Ontario in early April, the spring break-up would soon follow. Then, not even the desperate makeshifts which pushed the troops through would be possible.

By April 22nd, close to three thousand militiamen had travelled around Lake Superior on the C.P.R. line. A month later, the final track had been laid and the last eastern unit to be sent to the North-West, the Montreal Garrison Artillery commanded by Caron's close friend, Lieutenant-Colonel W. R. Oswald, could manage the entire journey without any of the arduous diversions of their predecessors. The first three thousand could take pride in their achievement. Colonel Arthur Williams hardly exaggerated when he wrote the Minister: "You ought to feel proud of the manner in which all the troops performed the march by Lake Superior. It would do credit to the best organized regular force in the world & is worthy of note historically."[20]

Most of the exhausted troops stopped first at Port Arthur, where townspeople rushed feverishly to give the volunteers their first palatable meal in a week. Then it was on to Winnipeg.

Lieutenant-Colonel Jackson, reaching the city on April 2nd, found it in a turmoil of excitement. Instead of being able to report for orders, he discovered that he himself, was the only uniformed officer there, "inundated with telegrams, contractors and people from many parts of the country who came to urge the organization of various local bodies . . ."[21] Two days after his arrival and only a day before the first contingent reached Winnipeg from the east, Jackson got his orders. He was to organize a commissariat corps, create a staff and take responsibility for all supplies, transport and pay arrangements for the campaign. On April 6th, he also learned that he was to assume the duties of Colonel Houghton as staff officer for the military district.

It was a staggering task. Jackson had never been popular with his Militia department superiors. There was a snobbish prejudice against his old occupation, a Brockville harness maker. Politicians never forgot that he owed his staff appointment to the Liberals. This background hardly made an almost impossible task easier. About the only major resource available to Jackson was the Hudson's Bay Company. With an unrivalled network of trading posts and stores throughout the Territories,

Joseph Wrigley, commissioner for the Hudson's Bay Company in Winnipeg. Fresh from Huddersfield, Wrigley took over the company's affairs at a difficult moment in its history. His contribution to the Canadian campaign has gone almost unrecognized.

with a transportation system that included steamers, barges and teamsters, the Company's services were available to the government—at a price. Its trade commissioner at Winnipeg, Joseph Wrigley, was a Yorkshireman not long in Canada but with all the qualities of integrity and caution which usually seemed to mark the senior officials of the company.

Even before the Duck Lake clash the government had arranged, through Colonel Houghton, for the Hudson's Bay Company to supply the small body of militia it planned to call into active service. After Duck Lake it was apparent to Wrigley that a much greater military effort would be organized; that a far greater demand for supplies could be expected. How many men would be sent and for how long? How much food were they to be given and what did the government expect to pay? With the end of winter approaching, stocks in the Company's storehouses were depleted and much would have to be ordered. Pestered for answers to these questions, Caron was immediately suspicious. Was he to be held responsible for over-ordering? How could he know how many troops would be needed? Was the Company taking advantage of him? Would the Liberals charge him with giving the Company special favours? These were fears accentuated by the outspoken hostility of the smaller Winnipeg merchants towards their big rival. On March 24th, Dewdney had warned that "public feeling strongly recommends that patronage to some extent be distributed when possible." The local Conservative M.P. reported "grave dissatisfaction."[22] "Orders for supplies going to our opponents' friends," complained a local party stalwart. "Wish them to come through me."[23] As inexperienced in military crises as the government, the Hudson's Bay Company now added the pressures of political patronage to the myriad of its concerns. "We are buying outside as cheaply as possible with payment," Wrigley reported to Caron, "but find everybody anxious to make money."[24]

Surrounded by angry and dissatisfied local merchants, pestered by contradictory and confusing directives from Ottawa, the Hudson's Bay official had little time for Colonel Jackson. Armed with his new orders, the staff officer informed Wrigley that, henceforth, all requisitions would come through him, but as he had received no direct orders from Ottawa, he could not authorize the purchase of further supplies. In short, the entire supply operation would be halted. Fortunately, the impasse was only temporary. Wrigley angrily appealed to Caron and the necessary authority was soon forthcoming. "Fear trouble from want of military organization and apparent incompetence,"[25] Wrigley wired Sir Donald Smith, the Company's chief commissioner in Canada and, through his C.P.R. interests, a close confidant of the government. His poor impression of the government's officials could only have been reinforced by Ottawa's meddling in his arrangements to buy 100,000 pounds of canned beef from Armour & Co. in Chicago. "Beware of Chicago tinned meat," Caron telegraphed. "We have had information that it has been poisoned,"[26] However well meant, the warning left Wrigley in a quandary.

Hanging a side of beef. The troops were soon tired of their diet of canned beef but transportation problems made fresh meat a rare luxury.

What else could he feed the troops? Local cattle dealers were eager to supply beef on the hoof but fresh meat meant an enormous added cost in time and money. Having raised fears—on the basis of a rumoured Fenian plot—Caron then left the matter to the men on the spot. Armed with a report from the local government analyst, Jackson and Wrigley agreed that the canned meat would be distributed.

Once the uncertainty about Jackson's authority had been removed, Caron found himself obliged to authorize first a month's supply of rations and, soon after, a still larger reserve. In turn, Wrigley had to promise faithfully to satisfy as many as possible of the local patronage seekers. Some of the demands were channelled through Caron's colleagues. "Will you request Minister Militia to instruct Wrigley to give contract for biscuits and bread to Thomas Chambers," the Minister of Customs was directed, ". . . the man that has it now are [sic] Grits and bad ones at that."[27] Although the troops were to grumble bitterly about their monotonous diet of canned beef and biscuit, they could thank Wrigley for resisting a determined attempt on the part of Caron to make them eat pemmican: it would, the Hudson's Bay official warned, be very unacceptable."[28]

Arranging for food supplies was one of the most straightforward of Jackson's tasks. He also had to find a staff and meet the varied and insistent demands of the militia units already flooding into Winnipeg. The only other Militia Department official in the city when Jackson arrived was Lieutenant-Colonel A. J. L. Peebles, an elderly veteran of the 1870 expedition who combined the duties of local police magistrate with those of paymaster and storekeeper for the military district. Major Elzéar Lamontagne, another staff officer who arrived with the first contingent of artillery, became Jackson's deputy, while several former militia officers, now living in Winnipeg, volunteered their services. Two of them, Lieutenant-Colonels Peter Attwood and Thomas Scoble had been enthusiastic militia officers in Ontario before the land boom lured them to Manitoba and Jackson was delighted to make use of their experience. The provincial government immediately became hostile. The two, Caron was informed, had been active agitators for the Farmers' Union. By indignant ministerial order, the two men were promptly dismissed. Other officers from the East soon filled their places.

Other former officers with more acceptable credentials had better luck. Lieutenant Colonel Thomas Scott, a Conservative M.P. and veteran of the 1870 expedition, and Lieutenant Colonel W. Osborne Smith, a retired militia staff officer, were both authorized to raise infantry battalions at Winnipeg. Jackson's most perplexing task was to find clothing, equipment and rifles for these new corps and for the troops of scouts and local guards which both Caron and General Middleton

Troops of the Midland Battalion march through Winnipeg. For most of the militiamen, Winnipeg was an oasis after the terrible journey around Lake Superior, a chance for a good meal and a wash.

were authorizing across the prairies. Peebles' worn-out stores were of little help.

To meet the demand, ammunition, rifles, revolvers and all manner of clothing had to be purchased. The benefits of having the government's own cartridge factory at Quebec were clearly demonstrated when the little plant produced a million rounds in only ten days. As a possible replacement for the worn-out, obsolete Sniders, Caron ordered 10,000 new Martini-Henry rifles from Britain. Since the Department kept no such things in stock, boots, shirts and underwear all had to be ordered from contractors. What material there was in government stores often proved worthless. There were enough blankets, for example, but Colonel George Denison insisted that his men get three of them instead of the official issue of two because they were so full of holes. For some essentials, Jackson even had to arrange his own manufacturing; he set one Winnipeg company to work turning soda water bottles into military waterbottles.

The first contingents from the East paused in Winnipeg only long enough to rest, repair their equipment and, in the case of the artillery batteries, to buy additional horses. Then they started out again, up the rail line to join Middleton. The later battalions waited much longer before orders were received, sending them to their eventual destinations. To some extent, Winnipeggers were responsible for keeping troops in their city. Apprehensive about the Métis clustered across the Red River at St. Boniface, some citizens feared that rebellion would break out in their midst if all the troops departed. More to the point, local merchants appreciated the extra business. Unfortunately, the campsite assigned to the troops turned out to be a miserable and cheerless place, a muddy un-drained field near the Presbyterian College on Portage Avenue. According to the suspicious Colonel Denison, it was chosen only because a government supporter had rented the nearby stables to the Militia Department. With only tents to protect them from the cold and rain, already weakened by their exhausting journey from the East, the troops suffered considerably. After only a few days on the "Mud Flats" a third of Colonel Denison's men fell sick while Colonel Amyot of the 9th Voltigeurs blamed the two deaths in his battalion on the condition in the camp. Inevitably, the blame fell on Jackson. "Among so many employees, it is inevitable that there will be a few idiots," Amyot wrote to the Minister of Militia, "Jackson is one of them."[29]

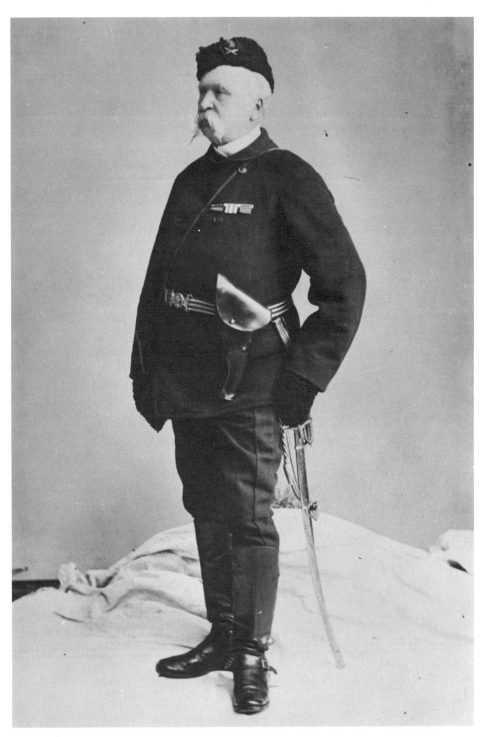

General Middleton dressed for the campaign. Having decried what he felt to be a Canadian militia propensity for full dress and feathers, Middleton felt he should set an example for sensible, inexpensive uniforms.

III. Fish Creek

While Jackson and Wrigley wrestled with their problems at Winnipeg, Major-General Middleton camped at Qu'Appelle, trying to organize his army and to devise a plan of campaign. Governor Dewdney and Superintendent W. M. Herchmer, the senior available N.W.M.P. officer, both came out from Regina to meet the General and he could learn a good deal about the country from them. However, there was no report from Prince Albert. Irvine, Middleton complained, "does not seem to think it necessary to give much intelligence."[1] Indeed, after only a few days in the North-West, the General rapidly developed a contempt for the mounted police which went hand in hand with a disdain for the military potential of his Indian and Métis opponents. Not that his own force was impressive. On April 2nd, after marching his men a few miles north to a new camp at Fort Qu'Appelle, he halted for a few days to give them some rifle practice. Middleton was a little disconcerted to discover that, in a force setting out to fight an enemy of reputedly crack shots, "many of the men had never pulled a trigger."[2]

For Middleton, however, even the inexperience of his troops was not his main problem: the greatest difficulty in campaigning across the vast and sparsely populated prairie would be transportation. The easiest solution, apparently, would be to use the rivers. For the past few years, paddle steamers along the branches of the Saskatchewan River had gradually been superseding the older method of freighting by waggon and two-horse team. Through a subsidiary, the Hudson's Bay Company operated a small fleet of steamers. So did Sir Alexander Galt's North-West Coal and Navigation Company, based at Medicine Hat. Both firms were delighted to rent their boats to the government for service during the emergency. The catch was that the steamers were still laid up for the winter and the bulk of the Hudson's Bay Company boats were at Saskatchewan Landing, near Prince Albert and behind the rebel lines. Moreover, navigation on the South Saskatchewan, a broad, winding, shallow stream,

Middleton's camp at Qu'Appelle. While Middleton planned his campaign, troops assembled, drilled and went through the unfamiliar exercise of firing their rifles.

depended precariously on the depth of the river. By the time Middleton could be ready to move, the small run-off from melted snow on the prairies would have gone down the river and water levels would fall until the heavier snowfall in the Rocky Mountains began to melt. Clumsy mechanical devices, resembling grasshopper legs, could be rigged to help the steamers over the mud flats but this was painfully slow work.

At the same time, land transport was not much easier. "These scoundrels have just selected the time when the roads will be almost impassable," Middleton reported to Caron, "the river the same and all the teams are required almost immediately for seeding."[3] Already, with winter breaking up, the snow had turned to slush and the notorious prairie mud would impede the passage of waggons and guns. It would be weeks before enough grass had sprouted on the prairie to allow the horses of the column to feed themselves; in addition to carrying the food, baggage and ammunition for the troops, Middleton's teams would have to pull their own forage. It was a desperately uneconomical prospect but if Middleton were to act quickly to end Riel's defiance before it had spread to every Indian reserve in the North-West, there was no alternative. Ironically enough, at about the same time that steamers would be able to move easily on the river, their cargoes of hay and oats would no longer be needed since, by then, the horses would be able to find grass.

To hire teams for his expedition, Middleton turned first to Archie McDonald, the Hudson's Bay Company factor at Fort Qu'Appelle. Settlers, choosing between teaming for a sure wage and the hazards of planting a crop, gladly hired on for $10 a day and all found. The biggest single contractor was the Qu'Appelle Valley Farming Company, a large, somewhat premature venture in commercial farming. Its manager, a former Canadian militia officer, Major W. R. Bell, had only just re-

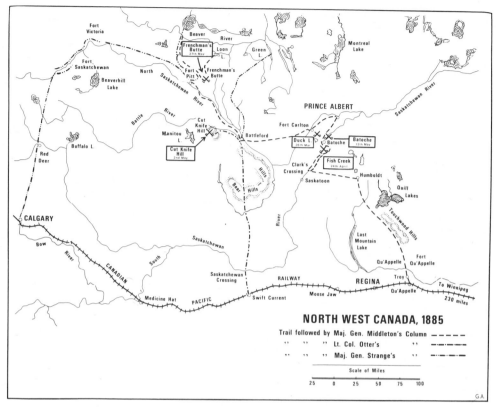

NORTH WEST CANADA, 1885

Trail followed by Maj. Gen. Middleton's Column — — — —
" " " Lt. Col. Otter's " —·—·—·—
" " " Maj. Gen. Strange's " —··—··—··—

Scale of Miles
25   0   25   50   75   100

turned from England at the outbreak of the rebellion. Delighted to find an officer and a gentleman in such circumstances, Middleton not only hired Bell's teams but appointed him quartermaster at Qu'Appelle, with orders to collect more waggons, teams and forage. He appointed a former British army officer, Samuel L. Bedson, the warden of Stony Mountain Penitentiary in Manitoba, to command the transport train.

Middleton's instinctive confidence in onetime British soldiers soon became apparent in the staff he organized for himself. When Lord Melgund arrived from Ottawa, the General promtly appointed him Chief of Staff. Captain John French, an ex-N.W.M.P. officer and the brother of Major-General Sir George French, was authorized to form a troop of scouts for Middleton's column. Major Charles Boulton, a Canadian who had held a commission in the British army as well as being one of Riel's prisoners at Fort Garry in 1870, received similar orders. There were, however, some former British officers whom Middleton did not want. He did his best to get rid of Colonel Houghton, describing him as "absolutely useless."[4] Caron chose to ignore the suggestion, leaving Houghton with the column to nurse the grievance that he, not Middleton, should have been in command. Another ex-British officer whose services Middleton preferred not to have was Major-General J. Wimburn Laurie. During long years in charge of the militia in Nova Scotia, Laurie had found

Major General J. Wimburn Laurie. Though desperately eager to crown his career with action, he was best known as an agriculturalist.

time to develop a prosperous farming estate and to give valuable service to the Conservative party. At the outbreak of trouble in the North-West, he hastened to offer his services but, with his British retired rank of major-general he would have superseded Middleton in seniority. Using this excuse and suspecting that Laurie would prove an embarrassment in the field, the War Office in London at first refused to allow him to serve. However, when the elderly officer agreed to ignore his seniority, the British authorities were obliged to relent while the Canadian government, mindful of past political contributions, "did not consider it advisable to refuse." This annoyed Middleton. "He will I am afraid be a nuisance and troublesome but I will try him."[5] The experiment did not last long. After spending a few awkward days in Middleton's camp, largely in the company of Colonel Houghton, Laurie was sent to Swift Current, a lonely little place which happened to be the closest point on the C.P.R. line to the South Saskatchewan River. Under the impressive title of "Commander of the Base and Lines of Communications," Laurie was to organize the loading of the river steamers.

In addition to imposing some unwanted staff officers on its field commander, the Canadian government also contributed advice. "I do not suppose that you will care to direct General Middleton's operations from Ottawa," Lord Lansdowne tactfully suggested to the Prime Minister but it was the Governor-General who remained one of the most persistent armchair critics of the campaign.[6] Through Melgund, his military secretary, he received regular and often highly critical reports of Middleton's doings. "I can not impress on the General the importance of securing line of communication,"[7] Melgund complained on April 3rd. In reply, Lansdowne returned to a theme he sustained throughout the North-West campaign: "I have always felt that it would have been a good thing if we could have dealt with this outbreak without sending the General to the front. His place at such a time is along side of the Minister here, and a younger man with more knowledge of military operations should lead on the spot. I am afraid you will have a deal of anxiety and trouble, but I am very glad you are with the Genl."[8]

While Lansdowne fussed and grumbled, his ministers waited and trusted. On the Sunday after the news from Duck Lake had reached him, the Prime Minister took the time to offer Middleton some of his "crude ideas" on the campaign. It really amounted to advice to do everything at once—to guard the railway, watch the frontier, arrange for the mounted police to organize local forces and, above all, to isolate the insurrection. A mounted force, Macdonald suggested, would be "nearly, if not quite, indispensable" and various troops of scouts had been and could be organized. "If you can get men enough from the Prairies, they would of course be much more serviceable than town-bred men who comprise our cavalry."[9]

The General accepted the advice about the eastern cavalry. Much to their disgust, Colonel Denison's troop from Toronto and Lieutenant-

Middleton's scouts. To the fury of cavalrymen from eastern Canada, the general preferred to recruit his scouts from prairie farmers.

Troops and waggons crossing a bridge near Qu'Appelle. Ignoring pleas for caution and delay, Middleton set out on April 6th, determined to strike at Batoche as soon as he could.

Colonel J. F. Turnbull's Cavalry School Corps stayed to guard the rear while hastily organized troops of settlers, on tough, prairie-reared horses, did most of the scouting for the militia columns. Other advice he disregarded. "The great danger is haste," warned Sandford Fleming, the eminent engineer who had helped lay out much of the line of the C.P.R., ". . . what is needed at the moment is not courage but a superfluity of caution."[10]

Middleton disagreed. Instead, even with only his scratch contingent of Winnipeg militia, he was prepared to march north to meet Riel. His reasoning was sensible. Delay would give the rebels confidence. It would also mean greater expense for the government and more time for the world to notice what was happening in the Canadian North-West. The best defence for the frightened white settlements was not to send them the troops and weapons which they demanded (which, in any case, Middleton did not have) but to strike out for the centre of the revolt, envelop it and deliver a knock-out blow. Middleton had accepted Dewdney's view that the entire rebellion depended on Louis Riel. If he and his stronghold at Batoche were captured, resistance among both Indians and Métis would collapse, Prince Albert and Battleford would be relieved and the campaign would be over. Any other strategy would be a waste of time and money.

On April 5th, Middleton at last received word that the first of the troops from the East, the permanent artillery battery from Quebec, had

passed through Winnipeg on its way to join him. Other men were close behind. His transport had been collected and his staff organized. Unless there were other reasons, he wired Caron, the rest of the mobilized militia might as well be kept in the East. The campaign was ready to begin.

On Monday, April 6th, Middleton marched out of Fort Qu'Appelle, leading his little force of Winnipeggers and a column of waggons that stretched for almost two miles. It took hard pulling to get the loaded waggons and the two guns of the Winnipeg Field Battery up the steep slope of the Qu'Appelle Valley but the men found it pleasanter than marching into the freezing wind that met the column on the open prairie. By the end of the day, the troops had covered a bare eleven miles. That night, it turned bitterly cold—at sunrise, it was 23 degrees below—and the shivering militiamen had to chop their tentpegs out of the frozen ground. For the next eleven days the march continued, passing through the Touchwood Hills to Humboldt and then west to Clarke's Crossing on the South Saskatchewan. It demanded from the Winnipeggers as much fortitude as the Easterners had shown on the north side of Lake Superior. Crossing the Salt Plains in the early spring meant that the infantrymen frequently sank up to their knees and even their waists in freezing water. On the treeless prairie, firewood had to be carried in waggons and the wet, half-frozen men were hard put to dry themselves. The General had left orders for reinforcements to follow as fast as they could and, from time to time, the column halted to allow them to catch up, By the time

Middleton reached Clarke's Crossing on April 17th he had been joined by 'A' Battery of the permanent artillery with a hundred men and two guns, part of "C" Company of the Infantry School Corps from Toronto, forty strong, and Major Boulton with his specially raised troop of mounted infantry. On the 18th, Lieutenant-Colonel H. J. Grasett and 250 men of the 10th Royal Grenadiers arrived, giving the General a force of 800 men and four guns.

While Middleton was marching overland to Clarke's Crossing, Lieutenant-Colonel Otter organized a supporting force at Swift Current. Composed of "B" Battery of the permanent artillery, the Queen's Own Rifles and the rest of "C" Company, Otter's column was to move down river by steamer just as soon as navigability permitted. Swift Current would then become the base for Middleton's force and the enormously expensive overland freighting operation between Qu'Appelle and Clarke's Crossing could be ended. Expense was a preoccupation with Middleton. "Everybody seems to think the Government fair prey,"[11] he remarked to Caron on April 8th. Once Otter's force had descended the river, Middleton would be able to concentrate more than 1,300 men against Batoche. By advancing along both river banks he would be able to surround Riel and his followers and bring their rebellion to a swift conclusion. Even Lord Melgund, whose spirits had risen during the march to Clarke's Crossing, now believed that there could not be more than 700 rebels and even that figure "must be exaggerated."[12]

Such concentration could only be achieved, of course, at the price of ignoring every anguished appeal from the beleaguered settlements in the north, even by disregarding what was virtually a direct order from Caron on March 31st to relieve Battleford. Middleton was now utterly convinced that the little town, with its host of frightened refugees, was quite secure. As for Prince Albert, he learned at Humboldt that it was safe. Although messengers from Irvine claimed to have run desperate risks in passing through allegedly rebel territory, Bedson, Middleton's Chief Transport Officer, and another man demonstrated that they could visit the town and return without any observable danger. On April 10th, however, Middleton and his men had their first news of the massacre at Frog Lake. Earlier, the General had ordered Superintendent Herchmer, with fifty police he had managed to collect, to march to the relief of Battleford. Finding the South Saskatchewan impassable, Herchmer had contented himself with deploying his men to protect the railway line and the laid-up steamers at Medicine Hat. The shocking news from Frog Lake forced Middleton to reconsider his plans. The tiny police detachment at Battleford just might not be enough protection for the five hundred men, women and children clustered within the walls of the fort. Accordingly, Otter's column at Swift Current received fresh orders to move, with all possible haste, to the relief of Battleford.[13]

Ferrying transport across the South Saskatchewan. Middleton split his force at Clarke's Crossing to be able to meet Riel on either side of the river.

Certainly the change in plan distressed Middleton. He blamed both Colonel Irvine and Inspector Morris, in charge at Battleford, for sending panicky messages. "Between ourselves," he suggested to Caron, "I believe they are both scared and unfit but I fear the chance of their being right."[14] Although he sorely missed Otter's five hundred men, Middleton felt strong enough to continue with the plan he had already adopted. He would divide his column and advance on Batoche along both banks of the river. It was a plan which broke one of the cardinal rules of textbook tactics—never to divide one's forces in the face of the enemy. However, Middleton had strong reasons. He was desperately anxious to prevent Riel and his followers from scattering. Moreover, the Métis village was built on both sides of the river and who could tell on which side, if either, the halfbreeds would meet him? To cross the river later, in the presence of the enemy, would also be difficult and very dangerous Moreover, the General could argue, each division of his force, 400 men and two cannon, was strong enough to deal with the entire rebel army. A signalling system could keep both columns in regular contact while steamers and barges on the river could transfer reinforcements from one side to the other. Despite doubts among his textbook-trained staff officers,

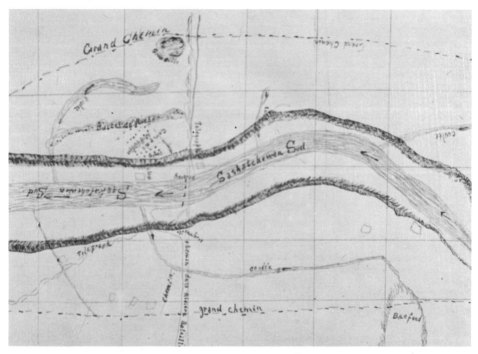

Among Riel's papers was found a sketch of Middleton's camp at Clarke's Crossing, forwarded by Jerome Henry, one of the general's teamsters. Another contemporary sketch of the camp helps illustrate Henry's topography.

Middleton persisted. Ernest Chambers, a young Montreal reporter who accompanied the column as a correspondent, later recalled that Middleton told him: "Some of these North-west people who are interested in keeping us as long as possible in the country for their own ends, and who are magnifying the difficulties of the situation for the purpose of bringing more troops and more money into the country would have us believe that there are thousands of half-breeds and Indians down the river, but I do not believe it."[15]

Lord Melgund was one of those who recorded his objections in a diary. He had, he believed, almost persuaded the General to transfer the entire force to the western bank of the river until Bedson pointed out the enormous labour of ferrying the waggon train, some two hundred teams and carts, to the other side. Even ferrying half the force took four days and a great deal of exhausting work. Only one leaky scow was found at the Crossing and another was borrowed from the settlers at nearby Saskatoon. Platforms had to be built, oars cut from wood, a wire rope rigged across the thousand-foot wide stream and a track built down the steep bank and past huge blocks of ice to the water's edge. The troops, faced with their first long delay since the march began, grumbled and criticized but they did their work.

On April 23rd the divided force resumed its march. Middleton, with the 90th, the permanent artillery and Boulton's mounted infantry, had remained on the east bank; across the river were the 10th Royals, the Winnipeg Field Battery and French's scouts, under the command of Lieutenant-Colonel C. E. Montizambert of the permanent artillery, with Lord Melgund as staff officer. There was still no sign of any steamer from Swift Current but Middleton could not wait. Loading the wire cable in the larger scow for future use as a ferry, he arranged for the clumsy craft to be floated down the river, the sole means of transportation between the two wings of his force.

At Batoche, Riel and Gabriel Dumont were still waiting, perfectly well informed of the movements of the militia. Indian and halfbreed scouts had been watching the column since it had left its base at Qu'Appelle and one of Bedson's teamsters, Jerome Henry, was a Métis spy, sufficiently adept to send Riel a plan of Middleton's camp at Clarke's Crossing. Despite his wound, Dumont was eager for another fight. He had planned to ambush Irvine's men as they retreated from Fort Carlton on March 27th but Riel had restrained him. Now he pleaded to be allowed to launch a series of harassing attacks after nightfall on Middleton's camp. It might have been a devastating tactic against Middleton's raw militiamen but Riel would not hear of it. It was too savage and, moreover, there was a danger that some of the French-Canadians might be hurt. Somehow, Riel had formed the impression that the French-speaking militiamen from Quebec were included in Middleton's column.

A sketch of the battlefield at Fish Creek by Captain H. de H. Haig, Middleton's quarter-master general. This was the view that faced Boulton's men when they approached the Métis ambush.

Dumont grumbled that he could see no harm in shooting down French-Canadians who had allied themselves with the English-Canadian oppressors, but, as usual, he gave way.[16] Instead, he accepted Riel's plan of fortifying Batoche. After all, Colonel Irvine and more than two hundred police and volunteers were only forty miles away at Prince Albert, ready, Riel assumed, to sweep down on the Métis headquarters at any moment. Indeed, on April 19th, as a result of a garbled message about Middleton's plans, the police commissioner did sally out at the head of his men, only to retire in haste when he discovered that the militia force was nowhere in the vicinity.

Eventually, neither Dumont nor his more ardent followers could wait any longer. On April 23rd, just as Middleton began to march north from Clarke's Crossing, Dumont and Riel assembled their most experienced and reliable Métis and Indian followers, two hundred in all, and rode south from Batoche. They had only gone a few miles when a messenger galloped up with a report. Irvine was out and heading for Batoche. Immediately, Riel and fifty of the Métis turned and rode back in haste to the settlement. The rest pushed on, past Gabriel Dumont's own farm toward Fish Creek. Their destination was a little stream, flowing through a deep and wooded coulee at right angles to the South Saskatchewan. The creek meandered across the floor of the coulee. Where it came close to the edge, the banks were steep and densely treed while the distant bank descended in a gentler, grassy slope. It was there that Dumont would make his first stand against the Canadian troops.

Dumont stationed most of his men in the coulee and along its northern edge, Indians predominantly to the right, Métis to the left. Tethering their horses to the trees near the creek bed, they set to work digging pits among the trees where they would be safe from the rifle fire and artillery of the advancing militia. Dumont, himself, took a small party of twenty horsemen forward of the coulee. As well as watching Middleton's movements, their task would be to draw the troops down the slopes into the gully. "I want to treat them like buffaloes,"[17] Dumont declared.

Middleton's column when the first shots were fired. This photograph is one of those taken by Captain James Peters during the battle.

By the night of the 23rd, the troops had marched eighteen miles from Clarke's Crossing. That evening, they found their first evidence of the nearness of the enemy when some of Boulton's scouts captured six Red River carts, loaded with barley and oats. The militiamen felt more confident now. Most of their early private fears about doing battle with a crafty and ruthless enemy—which had led many of the Toronto volunteers to arm themselves with revolvers and knives as well as their decrepit Snider rifles—had quietly evaporated when the Métis failed to put in an appearance. The exhaustion and misery of the early days of the campaign were also forgotten. The militiamen were now suntanned and fit and the weather was getting warmer. Soldiering, it seemed to them, could be a pleasant enough life—only a little dull.

Middleton's line of march had left the bald prairie. Now there were occasional homesteads and wooded bluffs. The trees meant welcome firewood but they could also provide an enemy with cover and the General increased his precautions, both on the march and at night. As usual, he personally visited the sentries after dark and, on the night of the 23rd, he spent a full two hours going the rounds, checking that each guard on duty knew his job. Not a man of them knew that Gabriel Dumont was barely half a mile away.

Next day the column was on the move by 6.30 a.m., with Boulton's scouts well spread out to the front, the General and his staff close behind and the main body about half a mile in the rear. On the other bank,

Montizambert's column made a slower start. With only a few waggons, it had even then run out of forage for the horses. With Middleton's troops already on the march, Lord Melgund was still busily trying to get hay loaded into the barge for transfer to his side of the river. He had barely returned from that errand when he heard shots from the other side.

Approaching Fish Creek, Middleton's advanced guard could see signs of recent enemy occupation. An English settler's house, its windows smashed, had been ransacked. Piles of grain lay on the ground, where horses had recently been feeding. Farther on scouts found abandoned camp fires with the embers still warm. The soldiers were therefore partially on their guard when, suddenly, shots rang out, raising puffs of smoke from a poplar bluff to the left of the advancing column. Dumont's advanced guard, perhaps panicking at the close approach of the scouts, revealed itself. At Boulton's command the mounted scouts turned and headed for the sound of firing. The Métis scrambled for their horses and dashed back over the edge of the coulee. Instead of following into the trap, the Canadian scouts dismounted and flung themselves on the ground as a hail of fire came at them from the concealed Métis and Indians. They returned the fire, convinced that they were holding back a horde of enemy from sweeping down on the main body.

Dumont's plan to trap the militia as it crossed Fish Creek had been frustrated by Middleton's careful deployment of his scouts. Now it was the General's turn to find out whether he could drive his opponents from their concealed positions. Men of the 90th Rifles and "C" Company advanced to the edge of the coulee and, in a series of unco-ordinated rushes, tried to make their way over the edge and come to grips with the enemy. Each time, accurate fire left casualties on the ground and drove the soldiers back. For their part, the only targets the troops could

Canadian artillerymen acting as infantry at Fish Creek. The troops lay a little back from the edge of the coulee, safe from enemy fire but hardly able to return it effectively.

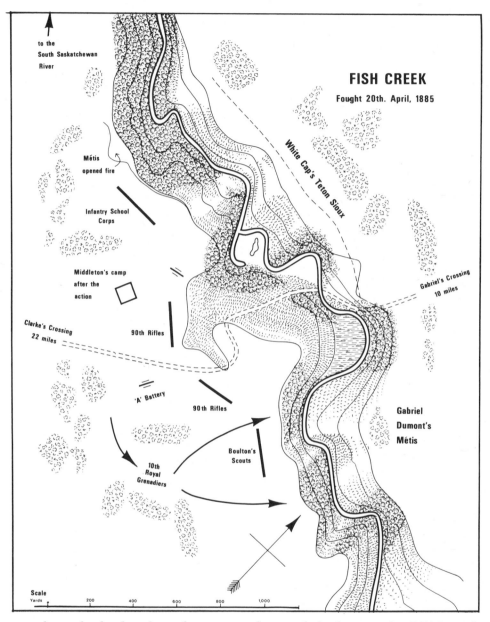

FISH CREEK

Fought 20th. April, 1885

to the
South Saskatchewan
River

White Cap's Teton Sioux

Métis
opened fire

Infantry School
Corps

Middleton's camp
after the
action

Gabriel's Crossing
10 miles

Clarke's Crossing
22 miles

90th Rifles

'A' Battery

90th Rifles

Gabriel
Dumont's
Métis

Boulton's
Scouts

10th
Royal
Grenadiers

Scale
Yards

200   400   600   800   1,000

see through the brush and trees on the creek bed were the Métis and
Indian ponies, helplessly tied to trees. They shot about fifty but it was an
expensive sport. Outlined against the sky as they craned over the bank,
the soldiers were an easy target for their enemies, hidden in the bush
below or standing, waist deep, in the creek itself. The two guns of "A"
Battery were unlimbered and pushed to where they could fire back but
artillery could not touch men hidden behind the near bank of the coulee;
the gunners had to be content with setting fire to the buildings of Mme.
Toureau's farm on the opposite side of Fish Creek. Here again, the

Métis marksmen revenged themselves: they found the artillerymen to be easy targets as they stood to load and fire their guns.

Time passed, with a cold wind whipping the clouds across the sky. Middleton was everywhere, moving with deliberate slowness, an easy and obvious target, his bulk giving added confidence to his nervous men. A Métis bullet tore through his fur cap. Both of his aides-de-camp, young graduates of the Canadian military college, fell severely wounded. Colonel Houghton, mounted on a conspicuous white horse, pushed so far toward the front that he inadvertently found himself the leader of one of the more impetuous rushes down the banks of the coulee. He escaped unscathed. So did Captain James Peters, whose permanent force gunners were fighting as infantry while their commander busied himself with taking the first battlefield photographs in Canadian history. Nevertheless the cool example of these few officers proved insufficient to persuade inexperienced and undisciplined soldiers to brave the fire of a concealed enemy. Middleton faced a stalemate.

So did Dumont, who also led a force of inexperienced fighters surprised and frightened by the artillery, dismayed at the failure of the plan to trap the soldiers and soon increasingly anxious to escape the battle. There was nothing in Indian or Métis tactical lore which called for prolonged

The battle of Fish Creek. This interpretation by the artists of the *Illustrated London News*, is more stirring, but perhaps a little less accurate than photographic records of the fight.

Men of the 10th Royals serving as a rear guard after the fight. Having gone to enormous exertions to get across the river, the Toronto men were dismayed to find that Middleton had decided to call it a day.

or desperate engagements and there was a great deal which suggested that each man be his own master. One by one, and then in small groups, the Métis and Indians began to slip away. Soon only the men in the centre, directly under Dumont's leadership, remained. Fearing that he would be outflanked, the Métis field commander and a few of his men headed up the creek bed and out on the far right of Middleton's position, to set fire to the prairie. The fire caught. Pushed by a favourable wind, smoke and flames rolled towards the militia, to whom it suggested a fresh and dangerous assault. Middleton, still cool, was not fooled. Calmly, he ordered the teamsters from his waggon train to go and put the fire out. Dumont, returning to his main body, found, by mid-afternoon, that he had little more than fifty men in the fight, some without horses.

On the west bank of the South Saskatchewan the other half of Middleton's army was almost helpless to intervene. In vain Melgund scouted the river bank to find a place where his two guns could be brought to bear on the Métis; they would have to be ferried over. It was not easy. Both banks were almost a hundred feet high while the shore was thick, sticky mud strewn with enormous blocks of ice. The barge, still full of hay and oats, could not be used at once. Somehow, it was unloaded; guns were lowered to be manhandled aboard. Again and again men rowed the overloaded craft across a river running at a determined four miles an hour. On the opposite side, the work of shoving the guns up the bank proved even harder. Nevertheless, three companies of Royal Grenadiers and both guns of the Winnipeg Field Battery crossed successfully while the battle was still in progress. Melgund went with the Toronto militia, all of them eager to display their prowess. The slackening fire from the valley suggested that a determined attack might now be successful and the newcomers were desperate to try. Middleton refused. Enough blood had been shed; he saw no point in needlessly incurring more losses. He would make camp. A first plan, to stop on the place of battle, was rejected as too dangerous. Instead the General sent Melgund to find another site, about half a mile away from the creek and closer to the river.

As Middleton prepared to withdraw, a force of eighty Métis, led by Edouard Dumont, galloped up behind the smoking ruins of Mme. Toureau's farm. The report of Irvine's attack on Batoche had been false. Edouard had come on as fast as he could to support his brother, picking up stragglers along the way. The soldiers, it seemed, were calling it a day so that this, if any, was the time for a final attack. The Grenadiers, who now formed the rearguard, eagerly faced about. But both leaders had decided that the battle was over. Middleton ordered the retreat to continue while Dumont collected his dead and wounded, before riding back to Batoche.

The battle had been something of a triumph for the Métis leader— only four of his men killed and another mortally wounded. In some ways, his most serious losses were the fifty-five ponies left dying in the coulee. Horses were a desperately important means of livelihood for impoverished Indians and Métis alike. On the other side Middleton's force had suffered six killed and forty-nine wounded, four of them mortally; and fifty-five casualties out of only 350 men engaged were heavy losses by any standard. In the retreat, two of the dead had been abandoned on the field.[18]

The weather in the morning had been brisk and sunny but a slow rain had begun in the afternoon and now, as the tired, dispirited men made camp, they were drenched by a sudden, heavy storm. As darkness fell, the rain turned to snow and the temperature plummeted. Few men could sleep. The black, dismal night seemed the perfect screen for Indian and Métis fighters, preparing to attack. While frightened sentries peered into the awful blackness, others tried to find warmth and shelter and to close their ears to the sounds from the tents where the surgeons worked. The men who had crossed the river with Melgund had come without their overcoats and blankets, and they suffered accordingly. "None of us are ever likely to forget the dark night of the 24th," Melgund wrote later, "close to the deep ravine, still holding for all we knew, a concealed enemy, and with us nothing but raw troops, totally unaccustomed to night work, and hampered by wounded men . . . We thought we had come out for a picnic, and it was impossible to help feeling that war's hardships are doubly cruel to the civilian soldier."[19]

IV. Batoche

The day after the battle at Fish Creek was a Saturday. Almost no one stirred from the militia camp. Middleton proposed going back to the battlefield to recover the two soldiers abandoned the day before but his officers dissuaded him. Perhaps the Métis still lingered there. Throughout the camp a pervading sense of gloom and despondency persisted and all that could be accomplished was to sew up the dead in their blankets and to ferry over the remainder of Montizambert's division from the far bank of the river.

Middleton had been badly shaken by his first encounter with the Métis. The self-confidence and disdain for his enemy which had so far governed his strategy had vanished. For almost a month the elderly general had displayed an energy and endurance remarkable for his years and weight. He had been everywhere and done everything—led the scouts, checked the guards—convinced that, as the only real professional in an army of amateurs, he must take personal responsibility for every detail. During the battle he had displayed an impressive, cool courage, exposing himself repeatedly to enemy fire in an effort to steady his men. Now his physical and emotional reserves were used up. Middleton was an exhausted man.

Suddenly he felt overwhelmed by the magnitude of what he had tried to accomplish—to lead utterly untrained and ill-equipped troops against men who had proved themselves to be as efficient and as resolute fighters as all the pessimists had predicted. "I could not help feeling sorry to see those poor citizen soldiers laying dead and wounded," Middleton wrote to the Duke of Cambridge, Commander-in-Chief of the British Army. "Most of them being well-to-do tradesmen's sons or in business and who thought they were going out for a picnic."[1] In a confidential letter to the Minister of Militia, Middleton acknowledged that his troops had behaved well in the face of the enemy but it had been "a very near

(top)
Sewing up the dead in their blankets. The discovery that men could be killed or suffer agonizing wounds brought an overdue realism to the minds of Middleton's men.

(bottom)
The General visits his wounded aides-de-camp. After the battle, Middleton was physically and emotionally exhausted. His confidence, which had grown steadily until the encounter with Dumont, evaporated.

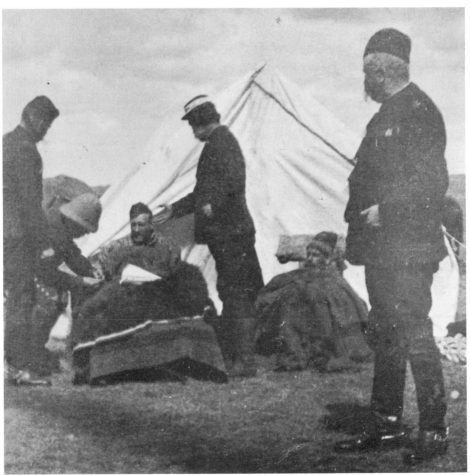

thing;" indeed, "if it had not been for myself and A.D.C.s it would have been a disaster." Any retreat would have turned into a rout and so he had been compelled to stand his ground. "When I had them in hand things became safe but I at once saw that with every inclination to do the best the officers were little or no assistance to me." Indeed, everything seemed to be conspiring to make difficulties for him: "Directly you leave the railway you are subject to all sorts of obstacles and delay. Creeks have to be crossed, bad roads to be passed, teamsters are troublesome, ferries won't run, panics seize the teamsters and they won't go without escorts. I am trying to do with as few troops as possible not only to save you money but to prevent the outside world thinking too much of it and thus injure the emigration."[2]

Now he must alter his plans for the campaign. Although Middleton might try to persuade himself and others that Fish Creek had been a victory for the militia, and that Dumont had lost heavily, he had become extremely reluctant to expose his men to further battles with the Métis. The force which had seemed to be utterly sufficient a week before, so sufficient that he was prepared to divide it in two, he now saw as "sadly less than we were and my men are nearly all without training and require managing."[3] The Métis, he told Caron, had prepared all the likely positions from Fish Creek to Batoche: "half a dozen men with lots of ammunition could kill a hundred or two men without difficulty and it would take a force of 5 or 6,000 men to turn them out."[4] Instead of continuing along the South Saskatchewan to Batoche, he would leave the river and march directly to Prince Albert.

Before he could do anything, however, Middleton had to resolve his transport problem. "Everything has to be carried in teams of 2 horses," he explained to the Duke of Cambridge, "and when you get to be 200 miles from your base, the team horses nearly eat what they carry."[5] Even at Clarke's Crossing, there had been a serious shortage of forage and at least some of the delay there had been caused by waiting for more to be brought up. Operating at the extreme range of horsed transport, the only solution was to add more teams. At Qu'Appelle, Major Bell had already arranged to hire 450 teams; he now appealed to Middleton for authority to take on 500 more. The General himself had attached 160 teams to his column for the advance to Batoche and those that remained on the route from Clarke's Crossing to Qu'Appelle were beginning to break down from the constant work. The whole business, with its unavoidable inefficiency, was extremely expensive. H. P. R. Street, a member of the government's Half Breed Claims Commission, learned that hay cost the government $20 a ton at Qu'Appelle but the round trip of twenty days to deliver it to Clarke's Crossing cost the government two hundred dollars. Moreover, since half the hay was eaten on the trip, each full ton that reached General Middleton would cost the govern-

The steamer *Northcote*. The logistics of the campaign, once the troops reached Clarke's Crossing, depended almost entirely on river steamers, but no one warned Middleton that navigation on the South Saskatchewan was still a risky and experimental business.

ment $440. With so much money to be earned there were rumours and allegations of corruption and favouritism, all of which were faithfully relayed to Adolphe Caron in Ottawa.

The only real solution, as Middleton had understood from the beginning, lay in using the rivers, but navigation on both branches of the Saskatchewan was still in its infancy, with promises much greater than fulfilment. On March 30th, Sir Alexander Galt had promised that his flotilla of steamers, designed to carry coal on the Belly River, could take the entire militia force from Swift Current to Prince Albert in four days "with exertion." However, it was not until April 27th that the first of the Galt steamers, the tiny *Minnow*, reached Saskatchewan Landing, near Swift Current. Meanwhile, the government had contracted to pay the full cost of fitting out the Galt steamers for the season and $250 a day for each of the boats from the moment they left Medicine Hat. The Hudson's Bay Company also had a steamer laid up at Medicine Hat— the *Northcote*. Its crew was already aboard when the rebellion broke out and it was able to make its way down to Saskatchewan Landing on the crest of the first run-off.

It was waiting there when Colonel Otter received his orders to move immediately to the rescue of Battleford. Middleton first directed Otter to travel by steamer to Clarke's Crossing, as in the original campaign plan, and then to march overland to Battleford. By this time, the river level had fallen and the other steamers had failed to make their promised appearance. As the ferry at Saskatchewan Landing had also broken down, the *Northcote* was pressed into service. It took the steamer four days to ferry Otter, 745 men, 400 horses and 200 waggons across the river.

General Laurie was now in command of the arrangements at Swift Current, an acutely disappointing end for the career of a soldier who had sought in vain, throughout his lifetime, for the excitement of active service. Moreover, Laurie was temperamentally ill-suited to dealing with contractors, teamsters and riverboat captains. Americans formed most of the steamer crews, men not easily reconciled to the pretentions of elderly retired British army officers. Some of them, with their own memories of Indian wars below the border, had little enthusiasm for risking their lives for the sake of Canada. Captain Sheets of the *Northcote,* for example, made it clear that his sole interest was in getting to Prince Albert to pick up his own ship, the *Northwest.* It took a direct order from Wrigley to impress him with his new responsibilities to the military authorities. There was a further delay while the steamer's boilers were cleaned. Then the *Northcote* had to be loaded with hay, oats, food, part of the field hospital, two companies of the Midland Battalion under Colonel Arthur Williams and one of the two Gatling guns the government had purchased at Middleton's request. Finally, on April 23rd, the ship left Swift Current. Captain Sheets predicted that it would take him only four days to reach Middleton; it took him fourteen.

Middleton, meanwhile, had not stirred from his camp at Fish Creek. Slowly, both he and his men had recovered their spirits, especially after scouts, venturing forth on the second day after the battle, reported that Indians and Métis were nowhere to be found. Soon, both Middleton and his men strained to be moving. Around the campfires, troops bluntly condemned their commander for his apparent lack of confidence and energy. In fact, Middleton was in a quandary. He could not leave his wounded unprotected nor could many of them be moved safely. Daily he expected the arrival of the *Northcote* with its medical assistance, reinforcements and supplies. Each day, it failed to appear. As time passed, any benefit of his rapid advance and even any possible dividends from the encounter at Fish Creek were being sacrificed. Farther west, Middleton decided, both Colonel Otter and General Strange were mismanaging matters. Laurie at Swift Current was no better. Middleton's only satisfaction came from kicking the reporter for the Toronto *Globe* out of his camp. The young man, a graduate of the Canadian military college, had had the temerity to criticize the soundness of Middleton's dispositions. The General's growing frustration burst out in his reports to Caron: "I am losing all advantage of having driven them off by this delay, and I can't move until my wounded are removed and this cannot yet be done until steamer arrives. Though I have enough to go on with,

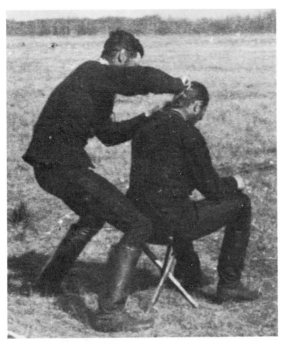

As the troops waited at Fish Creek, the monotony of their routine and perhaps the warmer weather revived their courage. Soon they were blaming Middleton for moving too slowly.

still I ought to have more ammunition which is also in steamer. I find this South Branch has only been navigated as an experiment which proved a failure and I ought to have been informed of this."[6]

In Ottawa, the Minister could do little. Unfamiliar with the North-West and with the complexities of military administration, he had a hard time even understanding Middleton's difficulties. His instinctive reaction seems to have been that someone was robbing the government and yet, he wired Wrigley, "There must be no mistake about supplies," "troops must be provided for and in good time."[7] To deal specifically with the transportation problem, he had already appointed Lieutenant-Colonel Edward A. Whitehead, a Montreal businessman and a former commanding officer of the Victoria Rifles, to serve as chief transport officer in the North-West. Whitehead arrived at the height of the transport crisis, at a time when more and more teams were being hired to operate on the hopelessly uneconomical route to Clarke's Crossing. Regarding the entire transport operation with a businessman's eye, he grew intensely scornful and suspicious of arrangements made a month earlier when conditions had been very different. Wrigley, whose company had arranged much of the hiring, fell under Whitehead's suspicion. The Hudson's Bay Commissioner now found that he had yet another officious military authority to contend with at a time when he was still being prodded from Ottawa to meet all of Middleton's demands.

The main problem was still the river. The heavy-laden *Northcote*, even with a draft of less than three feet, struck repeatedly on the mud banks. Middleton remarked later that she came "mostly by land."[8] When the *Minnow*, which drew less than a foot of water, arrived, Laurie decided to send her in pursuit. The little steamer could tranship the field hospital, ammunition and Gatling gun which Middleton urgently wanted and rush them up to the camp at Fish Creek. Laurie reckoned without the captain of the *Minnow*, an inebriated incompetent who dawdled down the river and who arrived at Clarke's Crossing a full five days after the *Northcote*. The *Minnow* had towed barges from Medicine Hat but, for the sake of speed, she soon abandoned them. Indeed, the captain suggested, they could travel downstream by themselves almost as fast as the steamer could tow them. When they had been loaded with supplies, their crews went on strike, refusing to start without a strong military escort. Laurie dismissed the men and manned the barges with eager volunteers from the Midland Battalion under Lieutenant J. L. Weller, another military college graduate.

The desperate need to get river navigation started led to an even more ambitious project. A Winnipeg firm, Boyd and Crowe, offered to build barges which, it was promised, could each carry twenty tons from Swift Current to Clarke's Crossing in from four to six days. With Wrigley's recommendation, the offer was accepted. On the evening of April 30th, a special train left Winnipeg, laden with lumber, tools and workmen to do the job. Waggons were specially collected to carry the men and material the twenty-five miles from Swift Current to Saskatchewan Landing. Within a week, eight of the barges had been built— and enough wood was left over to build two more. The next problem was to get them down the river. The contractors demanded twenty soldiers per barge as a combination escort and crew. Laurie made the counter-claim that the contract compelled Boyd and Crowe to provide the crews and that General Middleton had forbidden any transport train to be accompanied by a military escort. The eventual solution was to dismiss the civilian crews altogether, apart from one navigator per boat.

Men of the 7th Fusiliers from London were all too eager to put up with the work and discomfort of manning the barges if that meant that they could thereby reach the front. In the excitement, the humble task of delivering canned beef and oats to Clarke's Crossing was all but forgotten. Neither officers nor men knew anything about piloting barges and, at first, something of a holiday spirit prevailed. Laurie, trying to oblige the barge crews to stay together, ordered that all the rations for the men would be placed on one barge but river currents and mud flats soon dispersed the flotilla. Oars, crudely made from boards and green saplings, bent and broke and there were no tools to repair them or to make new ones. As men struggled in the water to free their stranded craft, the light-hearted mood drained away. Cargoes were jettisoned or dumped on the shore and, by the time the would-be sailors had reached their destination at Clarke's Crossing, the remainder of their freight was no longer needed.[9]

After half a month of waiting, Middleton's impatience got the better of his doubts. He would move without the *Northcote*. Arrangements possible days earlier were now made. Improvised stretchers made from the hides of slaughtered cattle were rigged on waggons, and those wounded who had survived the improvised field hospital set off for Saskatoon. There Dr. Roddick met them with a small medical detachment which had travelled overland from Swift Current. The former army surgeon and Victoria Cross winner, Dr. C. M. Douglas, outpaced Rod-

Captain A. L. Howard and his Gatling Gun. Though the primitive machine gun was not particularly effective in action, the fact that an American officer was with the column made Howard the central figure in many journalistic accounts of the campaign.

Scouts on the look out. After a few weeks at Fish Creek, Middleton resumed patrols toward Batoche and Prince Albert, satisfying himself that the Métis had not prepared a series of delaying actions along his route.

dick to Saskatoon by only a few hours. Travelling alone by canoe from Saskatchewan Landing, he had covered more than two hundred miles of river in less than five days. On May 2nd, Bedson set out with fifty teams to try to find the *Northcote* and relieve her of the more urgently needed parts of her cargo. On the same day, Middleton took Boulton's troop on a personal reconnaissance to within a few miles of Batoche. His journey convinced him that his fears of a series of Fish Creeks along the river bank were groundless. He was still reconnoitring when, on May 5th, he learned that the *Northcote* had at last arrived.

The campaign could now be resumed in earnest. To provide himself with some diversionary effect in his attack on Batoche, Middleton ordered that the little steamer be made defensible; timber, feed sacks, even a billiard table taken from Dumont's house, helped fortify the *Northcote*. Men from the permanent force infantry, under Major Henry Smith, were embarked as a fighting force. The new arrivals from the Midland Battalion made up for this detachment and for the casualties at Fish Creek although, a little unreasonably, Middleton complained to Caron that only half the battalion had been sent on. "Who interferes with your plans?" answered the Minister, "If you tell me, I shall put a stop to this."[10]

After a delay of more than two weeks, on May 7th, Middleton's reunited column at last marched out of its camp at Fish Creek. He now

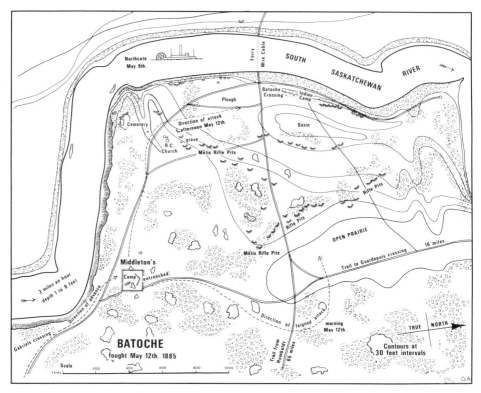

had about 850 men, four guns and a train of 150 waggons. The Gatling gun was under the charge of a former United States Army officer, Captain A. L. Howard, a veteran of Indian wars below the border. Another officer who had arrived in the *Northcote*, Lieutenant-Colonel Bowen van Straubenzie of the militia staff, had been a major in the British army. In keeping with his preference for that kind of experience, Middleton put him in command of the infantry of the column, to the indignation of Canadian officers of greater seniority in the militia.

After moving along the river to Gabriel's Crossing the column struck inland, avoiding possible traps and remaining on the open prairie. It made good progress and, that night, the troops camped six miles from Batoche. On the following day the camp was shifted only a few miles to a better protected spot about a mile from the edge of the bush which surrounded the approaches to the Métis village. The General spent most of the day with his mounted men, examining the approaches. That evening, he assembled his senior officers to announce his plans.

At Batoche, the South Saskatchewan made a very big bend to the west, coming back to the east side of the valley a mile or so below the settlement. The prairie cut straight across the bend, leaving a roughly shaped rectangle of lower land. On higher ground, at the south western corner of the rectangle, the missionaries had built a church and their seminary and established a cemetery. Farther along the river bank, a hundred and fifty feet above the water, a small, bush-filled ravine cut its way up to the height of land. The village, itself, consisting of a few stores and houses, was located on both sides of a much larger ravine, about half way up the western edge of the bend. The ravine led down to a cable ferry. A store and a few houses on the other side of the river were also part of the community and it was on the western bank, indeed, that Riel had first established his headquarters and raised his special white flag.

Since Duck Lake, most of the efforts of the Métis had been devoted to fortifying the village. Riel and Dumont had differed on how it should best be done, the latter insisting that the main defences must be to the south of the village, near the Catholic church, where the main trail ran. Riel preferred that defences be laid out to protect Batoche from all directions and, as usual, his opinion prevailed. Roughly three lines of rifle pits had been ingeniously constructed, proof against even artillery fire, and carefully hidden in the bush and scrub which covered the slopes leading from the village. Fields of fire had been carefully cleared so that the defenders would have a view of any approaching troops. It may not have been wise for the Métis and Indians to have spent so much time on the defensive, but their work had been ably done.

Certainly Middleton had no idea of the nature or location of the Métis' protective measures. His plan was simple, as perhaps was best with in-experienced men. At 6 a.m. on May 9th, the column would advance with Boulton's scouts, already familiar with the ground, leading the way through the dense bush until they rejoined the main trail. The infantry, with the 10th Royals in the lead, and the artillery, would follow. French's

A Métis rifle pit. Although the Métis might have been better employed harrying the approaching militia, their fortifications at Batoche had been skillfully and carefully constructed.

Rifle Pit

House with a White Flag (Riel's Ensign) flying.

Trail to Duck Lake, 5 miles.

Ferryboat.

Batoche's House.

Hollow where the Indian and Half-breed Camp was.

House where Prisoners were confined.

Batoche.

A panorama of Batoche. As sketched by Captain Haig, this was the view of the settlement from the church and priests' house, the farthest point reached by the militia on May 9th.

scouts were to bring up the rear. The camp would be left standing. By 9 a.m., Middleton expected to be approaching Batoche and the fighting, if any, would begin. There was only one stratagem to relieve the simplicity of the plan. By prior arrangement, the *Northcote* was to come down the river to reach Batoche at the same time as the troops. The Métis would find themselves attacked from two sides at once.

Well before dawn, Middleton's men were up and on the move but they had not reached Batoche when sounds of furious firing were heard, with the noise of a steamboat whistle blowing "for all she was worth." Dumont had been waiting for the *Northcote* with a surprise of his own.

The steamer *Northcote* under fire. This somewhat fanciful artist's impression records what some enjoy calling the first naval battle on the Canadian prairies.

The Métis had hauled the wire ferry cable out of the water and stretched it across the river at a height which would catch the boat and force it to surrender. As a result of confusion over the time, the steamer rounded the bend in the river at 8 a.m., an hour before Middleton's troops could appear. Almost at once, both the soldiers on board and the Indians and Métis on the bank opened a vigorous but largely ineffective fire on each other. Meanwhile Captain Sheets, in the unprotected little box of a wheelhouse on the top deck, watched helplessly as the wire rope swung toward him. There was a crash, the sound of splintering wood and a shower of sparks. The steamer heeled over as its mast, funnels and steam whistle were wrenched to the deck. The *Northcote* kept going. Dumont's wire had been stretched just a little too high. Indeed, not even Major Smith's orders could stop the ship: she kept going until there was a good two miles between her and Batoche. When she finally stopped, Smith stormed to the bridge. The *Northcote* must go back. Sheets and his pilot refused; they had had enough of being shot at. Smith found a volunteer to take their place but now the engineer informed him that he would not take the new man's orders. Smith had no choice but to continue down river toward Prince Albert. "Our weakness," he reported scornfully, "lay in the fact that the Master, Pilot and Engineer were aliens,

and that the crew were civil employees and not enlisted men."[11] Throughout the fusilade only two men, both of them civilians, had been wounded.

The *Northcote* diversion had served at least some of Middleton's purpose; he and his men managed to approach within half a mile of the Catholic church south of Batoche before they sighted their first Métis. Immediately, the artillery went into action, unlimbering their guns and opening fire. Sighting a few people near the church, Captain Howard loosed off a few bursts from his Gatling in their direction. Then, noticing that a white flag was flying from a house near the church, the column moved closer to find three priests, several nuns and some of the women and children of the settlement. By moving closer, the gunners were also able to begin shelling Batoche itself, as well as houses on the other side of the river. While they paused to do this, Dumont's men had a chance to recover. They had spent too much time congratulating themselves about driving off the *Northcote* but Middleton's cautious advance gave them the time they needed to re-occupy their prepared positions.

Very soon, much the same situation as at Fish Creek was reproduced. From the high ground around the church, Middleton's infantry tried to come to grips with a hidden enemy. Once again, troops exposed on the high ground were easy targets for Métis and Indian marksmen concealed in the bush below. Militiamen who tried to advance were sharply punished. The clumps of bush and the sharp dips in the ground isolated the troops and increased their susceptibility to panic. They also helped cover the approach of small groups of Dumont's men, this time far more aggressive than at Fish Creek.

As on the morning of Fish Creek, Middleton soon appreciated that he was in an extremely unpleasant position. He had no idea of what

Instead of continuing the advance toward Batoche, Middleton chose to begin his attack with an artillery bombardment by his four guns. Captain Peters was on hand to record the scene. He also photographed the smoke from a prairie fire, probably started by the Métis in an attempt to cut off Middleton's line of retreat.

Middleton's troops at the priests' house. The Canadians had stopped at the edge of the clearing and opened fire, only to discover that they were bombarding the refuge of the remaining Catholic priests and nuns and a few Métis women who had taken refuge with them.

had become of the *Northcote*. His infantry were now fully extended, the Grenadiers to the right, facing north toward Batoche; the 90th lining the river bank and the cemetery, trying to keep the Métis from infiltrating around the steep and wooded slope, while the Midlanders were busy clearing the steep gully near the church. One aggressive group of Métis almost managed to rush one of his guns. The infantry could only be pushed forward with the certainty of heavy losses and it had been dangerous work merely to rescue those wounded who had fallen in exposed places. The deep coulees and bush could make it possible for the Métis to cut through and divide the force. Already reports had reached the General that the 90th could not keep infiltrators from moving around the river bank and prairie fires to Middleton's right might also indicate a flanking movement.

In hurried, anxious tones, Middleton and his chief staff officers conferred. Melgund, Van Straubenzie and Captain H. de H. Haig, an officer from the Royal Engineers who had been serving as Middleton's Quartermaster General, came to one conclusion. The only safe course was to withdraw to the camp they had left standing that morning. This did not convice Middleton. Could his shaken troops muster the discipline and skill required for such a withdrawal or would retreat turn into panic-stricken flight? Moreover, his Canadian officers, less familiar with formal military doctrine, could not see that they had been defeated. Dr. George T. Orton, a Conservative M.P. who was serving as senior surgeon with the column, and Colonel Houghton later claimed joint credit for persuad-

Dr. George T. Orton M.P., Middleton's chief surgeon. In later years, Orton claimed that it was his insistence that the wounded could not be moved which prevented the General from ordering a retreat.

ing the General to stand firm. Months later, Orton recalled that he had told Middleton: "I did not think there was a volunteer officer or man under his command but who would rather die on the spot than retire a mile . . ."[12]

Whether or not he was moved by Orton's oratory—or even had a chance to hear it—Middleton made up his mind to stay. He sent Boulton and his scouts back along the trail to escort the waggon train to a new site about a mile from the Métis entrenchments. There, the waggons, formed into a square protected by shallow trenches, became a "zareba" as the current military jargon termed it. It was there the Canadian troops spent their first night at Batoche. The Métis cautiously pursued the soldiers to their new camp but at dusk most of them withdrew. Nevertheless, the troops regarded the disappearance of their enemy as a prelude to a night attack and most of them remained on guard during the hours of darkness. Nothing much happened. A few stray bullets from the surrounding bush managed to wound one man and kill two horses. In the first day of fighting, total military casualties were two killed and ten wounded.

Late on the afternoon of that first day, Lord Melgund left the column alone, riding across country toward Humboldt. It was clear evidence of the seriousness of affairs that Middleton should have sent away some-

Canadian officers resting in the "zareba." After a first sleepless night, Middleton's men settled down to the routine of besieging Batoche. Their own fortifications were simple in the extreme.

one he described to the Duke of Cambridge as "the only man I can trust."[13] Melgund's diary, perhaps intended for future publication, merely commented that the General had asked him to carry some messages and to go to Ottawa "for several reasons."[14] The real reason, as some in the force soon guessed, was that both Middleton and Melgund now feared a debacle; if it occurred, there was no point in losing both men. Should Middleton and his force be cut to pieces, Melgund would be available to command a relieving force, almost certainly built around regular troops of the British army. By the morning of the 10th, Melgund reached Humboldt to find Lieutenant-Colonel George T. Denison and his Toronto cavalry encamped. Denison, a man of many grievances against British professional soldiers, doubtless took some small private pleasure in the news that Middleton, though not defeated, had suffered a check.

Melgund's official reports, telegraphed from Humboldt, were firmly optimistic, but his confidential comments to the Governor-General were much less reassuring. For the second time, Lord Lansdowne's anticipation of disaster approached the edge of reality. Middleton, he informed the British Colonial Secretary: ". . . was obliged to camp on very dangerous ground & that if the rebels do not disperse, but renew the attack, he is likely to be hard pushed & may have to retire to the open prairie.

I take it that he would have done this had he not dreaded the effect of a 'strategic movement to the rear' after an indecisive action."[15]

In later years, commenting on his campaign, Middleton sought to leave the world with the impression that he had deliberately conducted a wearing battle at Batoche, seeking to tire out Dumont's men and to train his own. In fact, he does not seem to have known really what to do. On the 10th, a Sunday, he marched his men out to the same positions they had occupied the day before. Again confused and desultory encounters with the Métis occurred in the bush and ravines south of Batoche. The price for the day's operations was one man killed and five wounded, suggesting, Middleton later claimed in his report, "that the men were improving in their fighting."[16] On the same day he ordered Captain French and a few of his men to ride north, to find an open plain which reportedly might offer a fresh approach to Batoche. They found it and hurried back to camp to report. Reinforcements also began to arrive—fifty men of the Dominion Land Surveyors. That night there was more confidence in the camp, and probably a good deal more sleep.

Next morning, the 11th, the infantry again marched out to their familiar positions while Middleton, most of his senior officers and a strong escort of mounted men, set out to look at the large clearing French had located the day before. About a mile from the camp they reached it, a wide, level plateau which ran unobstructed all the way to the edge of the river valley. On the far edge was a line of rifle pits. This approach, too, was defended. The reconnaissance continued with a chase as Middleton and his scouts galloped after two mounted Indians. They escaped easily but Middleton, singlehandedly, captured his own prisoner, an unarmed elderly Métis searching for his cattle. After setting a few log huts on fire and rounding up all the stray horses and cattle they could find, the Canadians rode back to camp. The infantry, too, returned. Once again they had suffered casualties—one killed and a few wounded —but their confidence was rising and turning to impatience.

Middleton still had not found a way to win the battle. That evening, he formally called for help. "Am in rather ticklish position," he wired Caron, "Force can succeed [in] holding but no more—want more troops."[17] The Minister's response was immediate. A second mobilization of militia units took place within hours. The Montreal Garrison Artillery, commanded by Lieutenant-Colonel W. R. Oswald, a close friend of the Minister, now received orders to proceed to the North-West and another Montreal battalion, the 1st Prince of Wales Rifles, was called out as a reserve. So were the 32nd Bruce Battalion in Ontario and a composite battalion of New Brunswick militiamen, organized around the permanent infantry school at Fredericton. Troops already in the North-West were directed to move closer to Batoche. O'Brien's York and Simcoe Battalion marched to Humboldt to reinforce Denison's cavalry while men of the 7th Battalion (who, unknown to Middleton, were struggling with their barges) were ordered to Clarke's Crossing. The rest of the Midland Battalion was summoned to join Middleton's column. Those were not the precautions of a complacent or even of a confident man.

By the end of their third day at Batoche, Middleton's men were getting fed up. Casualties had been relatively light. The troops were becoming acclimatized to the enemy's fire. The daily routine of advance, skirmishing and then retreat seemed pointless dallying. On the other side, the Métis were becoming discouraged. They had not been prepared for a prolonged siege, many of them were, at best, reluctant warriors, and ammunition was beginning to run short. Dumont could still depend on only a few hundred to man the defences and, on the 11th, many of the Métis who had been resisting the militia infantry south of Batoche had had to race across to the rifle pits on the east to meet the possible threat of Middleton's mounted reconnaissance. Throughout the weeks since Duck Lake, Riel had insisted that the government troops would be met only at Batoche but, now that they had arrived, there were few effective means of resistance.

Or, perhaps there was one possibility—the prisoners. Early on the morning of Tuesday, May 12th, Riel released two of his captives with a message for Middleton: if the General massacred the Métis women

The York and Simcoe Battalion marching to Humboldt. Reacting to his initial setback at Batoche, Middleton ordered supporting troops to move closer and asked Caron for reinforcements.

and children by continuing to shell the houses, the prisoners would all be killed. On the outside of the envelope, Riel himself scribbled "I do not like war," adding a further threat to kill his captives if Middleton refused to retreat and grant him an interview.

The two men, both paroled to return to captivity, met Middleton on the clearing to the east of Batoche. By this time, the General was a changed man. At last he had devised a plan to take the Métis stronghold. Part of it was already in operation. As on the previous day, he and the mounted men would ride out to the open plateau, this time bringing with them one of the guns from "A" Battery. Again the enemy would be drawn in his direction. Once they were fully engaged, the gun would open fire and the sound would be a signal for Van Straubenzie and the infantry, drawn up in their usual positions a mile and a half away, to advance. Early in the morning, Middleton had carried out his share of the plan. The Métis had been engaged, there had been a brisk exchange of fire, one of the land surveyors had been killed and the cannon had fired its shots. But, for some reason Middleton could not understand, the main body of infantry had not budged. Furious at the miscarriage of his plan, Middleton was returning from this abortive foray when he met the two released prisoners. He was not in a mood to be moved by their message. If Riel would place all the women and children in one place, under a white flag, the General replied, he would see that no shots were fired in that direction. As for Riel himself, only unconditional surrender would be acceptable although Middleton would guarantee to protect the Métis

French's Scouts at Batoche. To break through the Métis defences, Middleton planned a diversion with his small mounted force, drawing off Dumont's men so that his infantry could attack successfully.

Middleton takes a prisoner. On May 11th, the General "captured" an elderly Métis who happened to be out searching for his cattle.

leader's life until he was handed over to the government. Only one of the prisoners, John Astley, a surveyor, agreed to carry this uncompromising message back to Riel; the other, a brother of Riel's former associate, W. H. Jackson, preferred to break his parole and remain in safety with the troops.

Middleton's temper had not cooled by the time he returned to camp, and he was not mollified by the explanation that the sound of cannon fire had not been heard back at the zareba. In vitriolic language, Van Straubenzie was assured that he could dismiss his men to their dinners and, later, when they had reformed their ranks, that he could take the troops as far as he pleased. Middleton himself, his mounted men and the 90th Rifles proceeded to have their midday meal.

It seems obvious that Middleton merely intended that his infantry would return to take up their old positions near the church. The line was now formed with Colonel Williams and his two companies on the left, closest to the river, with Colonel Grasett and 200 of the Royal Grenadiers on the right and the 90th Rifles in the rear. What precisely happened next remains obscure, partly thanks to the conflicting claims of the more senior participants. Probably both Grasett and Williams had quietly made up their minds that there would be no turning back this time, while Van Straubenzie had been bitterly stung by some of the General's comments. The impetus may have been an order to Williams to swing his two companies, deployed between the cemetery and the river's edge, until they were abreast of the main line. As the Midlanders advanced, the movement became general. The whole line of infantry began to surge forward, broke into a run and poured down the slope, the men now cheering as they went. In a few minutes, they cleared the corner near the church of its few remaining defenders; then the militiamen raced headlong down the slope toward Batoche. The noise of troops cheering and firing hurried Middleton and the rest of his force from the camp.

The final charge at Batoche. While it may seem appropriate to preserve an heroic vision of the only real militia victory of the campaign, it may be unfortunate that Captain Peters had put away his camera.

Now the General struggled to regain control. First the 90th and then both the troops of mounted men set off to extend the flank inland, to prevent the attackers from being outflanked and cut off. The guns and ammunition waggons of "A" Battery and the Winnipeg Field Battery rushed forward to find their place in the advancing line. Dumont's men, caught by surprise, were still expecting an attack from the east, across the open plain. The few who had remained in the southern rifle pits were short of ammunition. They fired what they had and fled, though a few stayed, accepting certain death. The troops only encountered effective resistance when they reached the houses of the settlement. There, Captain French was shot, but the momentum of the onslaught could not be stopped by the few Indians and Métis who held out. Still, victory was not easily conceded and scattered firing continued until dusk.*

*It was on this occasion that Dr. George Sterling Ryerson, riding forward to collect the wounded of the 10th Royals, displayed Canada's first Red Cross flag on his waggon.

The day had cost Middleton five killed—four of them officers—and twenty-five wounded, but it also brought him the first and probably the only clear-cut victory of the campaign. For the first time, the Métis had suffered heavy casualties. Middleton's men found twenty-one dead and five wounded on the field although the Catholic parish priest reported that, in the four days of fighting, fifty-one Indians and Métis had died, all but four on the final day.[18]

Most of the Métis women and children were found where they had spent the siege, camped under the shelter of the steep river bank, north of the settlement. Part of Middleton's force spent the night camped among the ruined houses. Although the General and his officers later denied it, a letter from Major Boulton to his father reported that. "(T)here was a great deal of looting going on and whatever was worth taking was soon in the hands of the men and officers, consisting chiefly of furs that the rebels had left in the stores, saddles and all kinds of inconceivable things."[19]

To complete the triumph, towards 6 p.m. a steamboat whistle announced a welcome arrival. The *Northcote* hove in sight, towing the *Marquis*. After the crew's refusal to turn back on the 9th, Major Smith had gone on to Hudson's Bay Ferry, directly to the south of Prince Albert where he found the *Marquis* and a police guard sent by Irvine. Middleton's last instructions, Irvine pointed out, were that he and the column were proceeding directly to Hudson's Bay Ferry and expected to be met. Smith fortified the *Marquis*, placed the police detachment aboard as a guard and set off for Batoche early on the 12th. Had the *Marquis* not damaged her steering gear, the little flotilla might have arrived in time for the battle.

For Middleton, only one thing more was immediately necessary: to capture Riel. "I am ready to receive you and your council," the General promised the Métis leader during the battle, "and to protect you until

Dead Métis at Batoche. Although out of ammunition, some Métis fought to the end, being shot by the advancing troops.

(top) Louis Riel, a prisoner in Middleton's camp. Although the General claimed to have captured the Métis leader, it is more accurate to say that Riel deliberately surrendered, under the illusion that he could vindicate himself in a great state trial. (bottom) One of the Métis dead, reportedly Alexander Ross, the man who had killed Captain John French.

your case has been decided by the Dominion Government."[20] Another copy of this message was sent out in the hands of a released Métis prisoner on the 13th. Riel had fled from Batoche with Dumont and other loyal supporters, but he had no intention of either carrying on the fight or of seeking refuge in the United States. Confused, tired and badly frightened by the fate that might await him at the hands of the Ontario soldiers, Riel had made up his mind to surrender himself and to continue his struggle in another arena. To Dumont it seemed an absurd and quixotic notion, but he never could argue successfully with his leader. At last, and very sadly, Gabriel Dumont had to leave Riel and save himself. Skilfully evading the police and military posts set up to capture the fleeing rebels, the old buffalo hunter eventually reached the relative safety of the United States. As for Riel, on May 15th, two of Boulton's scouts, accompanied by Tom Hourie, Middleton's Indian interpreter, found him near the main trail to Guardepuis Crossing. Armed only with Middleton's safe conduct, he had come to surrender.

V. Cut Knife Hill

While General Middleton and his men had been advancing to Batoche, two other forces had been busy. From Swift Current, Colonel Otter and 500 troops had marched north to the relief of Battleford while, from Calgary, another column under Major General Strange had been organized to move first to Edmonton and then eastward to Fort Pitt along the North Saskatchewan river.

In retrospect, it might be possible to assume that these movements represented the execution of a carefully conceived, highly co-ordinated plan. Nothing could be farther from the truth. No grand strategic vision illuminated General Middleton's mind beyond his sensible determination to deliver a single, concentrated attack on the centre of the rebellion. Other activities were diversions which he opposed in principle and in which he took little interest. He opposed the detachment of Otter to Battleford as long as he could and, as for Strange, he despised the man from the start and sent him militia battalions he did not wish to have under his own command. A commander who could not take effective steps to co-ordinate his plans with Commissioner Irvine at Prince Albert was hardly likely to preoccupy himself with more remote strategic combinations.

Determined to conduct a brief and economical campaign, Middleton chose to believe that the only significant danger was from Riel and his followers at Batoche. He firmly refused to detach troops to garrison defenceless prairie settlements if they were not on his lines of communication, or even to supply arms to the teamsters who drove his waggons. To do so would have meant postponing his own campaign until more arms and men were available. However, to frightened settlers, the halfbreeds seemed a much less immediate threat than the thousands of Indians scattered across the prairies. To the generations of myth and memory of Indian wars and massacres were added the recent violent history of the American frontier. The poverty, misery and degeneration of the Indians

Poundmaker, chief of the Cut Knife reserve. A man of imposing presence and a renowned judge and orator among his Cree people, he struggled in vain to hold back the young men of his band.

since their confinement on the reserves had encouraged the incoming white settlers to regard the native people with contempt and disdain. That attitude was swiftly transformed to terror when the Indians struck back—or appeared to have the power to do so.

The Indians had also been very much part of Riel's strategy. Métis emissaries kept in touch with virtually every band during the spring of 1885 and their influence was strengthened as news spread of the events at Duck Lake, Frog Lake and Fort Pitt. At Battle River and Lac la Biche, Hudson's Bay Company posts were plundered. In the Eagle Hills, Stoney Indians murdered a farm instructor and another white settler and moved to join Poundmaker's band of Crees near Battleford. It is the campaign against Poundmaker that will be considered next.

A big, strikingly handsome man, with a magnificent voice, Poundmaker was known among his people as a great judge and speaker and his influence extended far beyond the two hundred families of his band. However, it was influence, not power, that he possessed. Even more than Big Bear, Poundmaker's caution grew with his advancing years and, as the times of trouble approached, his prestige was not sufficient to restrain the younger, more turbulent members of his band. Generally ill-informed about the nature of Indian tribal democracy, white outsiders almost invariably overestimated the degree of control a chief exercised over his band.

The greatest threat which the Métis rebellion seemed to present to the Canadian government was the risk of it precipitating a general Indian uprising throughout the North-West. That danger lessened with the prompt arrival of militiamen from the East. Under Dewdney's management and authority, the mean-minded regulations of the Indian Department were ignored, extra rations were issued to the Indians and an emergency policy of present benevolence and future threats was instituted. It had its effect. Even those Indians like the Crees along the North Saskatchewan, who joined the rebellion, did so tentatively, waiting to see what would happen. Others, like the Woods Crees and the Chippewayans, who apparently went along, were in fact holding back. The Blackfoot confederacy of southern Alberta, probably the most powerful and warlike group of Indians in the Canadian North-West, played a crucial role. In 1884, they had also been among the most conspicuously discontented, and even before the battle at Duck Lake the government had begun to take precautions. Sir John A. Macdonald had arranged for Father Albert Lacombe, a highly successful Oblate missionary among the Blackfoot Indians, to use his influence on their leading chief, Crowfoot. For his part, Dewdney managed to obtain the help of C. E. Denny, a former police officer and Indian agent who had resigned in protest at the government's penurious policy towards his charges. Subjected to these personal pressures and with government assistance suddenly avail-

A Chippewayan camp. Though only a small proportion of the Indians on the prairies joined the 1885 rebellion, they aroused most of the terror which gripped the white settlers.

able to help his people, Crowfoot reaffirmed his loyalty. "We will be loyal to the Crown whatever happens," read a carefully dictated message to the Prime Minister, "I have a copy of this and when the trouble is over will have it with pride to show to the Queen's Officers and we leave our future in your hands."[1]

Pacifying the Indians was only part of the government's problem. Anguished messages flooded in from white communities on the prairies, insisting on protection. The Minister of Militia dealt with most of them by referring them to his commander in the field and, for the most part, Middleton simply ignored them, treating them only as evidence of the craven panic he found so widespread. In a few cases, Caron found that the appeals were backed by too much political influence to be completely put aside. The intervention of N. Clarke Wallace, M.P., seems to have helped win at least some protection for the York Farmers' Colonization Company's settlement at Yorkton. Two former British army officers, who happened to be in urgent need of a little income, were despatched to the little town, together with a shipment of rifles. There, they constructed a modest fort and drilled a home guard composed of settlers—at least until their military activities were found to be interfering inordinately with the Company's commercial purposes.

The Indians in the southern parts of the Territories might be cowed or won over but those along the North Saskatchewan were in open, if disorganized revolt. At Battleford, Inspector W. S. Morris, a former militia officer from New Brunswick, found himself in charge of eighteen police, two old cannon and a tumble-down fort, with responsibility for protecting more than five hundred refugees, over three hundred of whom were women and children. Six years earlier, an unsuccessful attempt had been made to organize militia companies in the North-West and the rifles for the non-existent units were still stored at Battleford. Using these weapons, Morris formed a volunteer company, the Battleford Rifles, and a larger home guard. Supplies were also found to be adequate for a prolonged resistance and ditches and embankments soon reinforced the defences.

The chief weakness of the defenders was psychological. Rationally, the fort was perfectly safe. The Indians had no practical experience of siegecraft and there were probably more rifles and able-bodied men to use them inside the fort than among the Indians prowling outside. However, the whites did not think so. At the very outset of trouble, two of their official leaders, Judge Charles Rouleau, the stipendiary magistrate for the district, and A. T. Berthiaume, the overseer of public works, had piled their families and what they could carry on carts and headed south for Regina. The white settlers who had stayed behind watched helplessly from behind the walls of the police fort while the Indians engaged in the leisurely destruction of the settlement, burning only a few houses each evening. Overcrowding in the tiny fort—measuring only 90 by 100 feet—did not help morale. The commandant's two-storey cottage billeted seventy-two women and children throughout the siege. Morris, obviously not a man of great daring, claimed that he could not sally out with his untrained followers without leaving the fort inadequately defended. In short, both settlers and police felt themselves to be in danger, a sensation which can hardly have been relieved when, on April 21st, Inspector Dickens and his men arrived to tell the story of Frog Lake and Fort Pitt.

Middleton had been perfectly confident about the safety of Battleford. Morris, he suggested to Caron, was typical of the kind of cowardly and incompetent officer who would have to be removed in any reform of the North West Mounted Police. Nevertheless, the news of Frog Lake had shocked the General as it had the whole of Canada, and it was almost wholly in response to that news that he ordered Colonel Otter north to the rescue. Otter was a Canadian-born officer, although sufficiently connected with the English gentry—two of his aunts had married into the peerage—to be of some interest for the inveterately snobbish Middleton. As an officer in the Queen's Own Rifles, he had been present as adjutant of the battalion at Ridgeway in June of 1866, when the Canadian militiamen had turned tail and fled before the Fenians. That experience had left its mark. Thereafter Otter devoted himself heart and soul to turning

Lieutenant Colonel William Otter. As a young man, he had seen the Canadian militia turn tail and flee at Ridgeway in 1866.

his unit into the best trained and most efficient in the Canadian militia. He had done so well that in 1883, as he was coming to the end of his term as commanding officer, Middleton's predecessor had selected him for a senior appointment in the newly-expanded permanent force. Unlike almost all the other senior officers in the North-West campaign, Otter had had no connection with the British army. He symbolized both the possibilities and the limitations of what Canadians could achieve within the narrow confines of their own service.

On arriving in the West, Otter had been ordered to proceed directly to Swift Current to organize the force which would accompany Middleton's column down the South Saskatchewan to Batoche. At Swift Current, he found Superintendent Herchmer and the fifty police who had originally been expected to relieve Battleford. In addition, there were 113 men and two guns from "B" Battery of the permanent artillery, 274 men of his old battalion, the Queen's Own Rifles under Lieutenant-Colonel A. A. Miller, 51 men from Captain Todd's detachment of the Governor General's Foot Guards from Ottawa and 49 men of Otter's own command, "C" Company of the Infantry School Corps. Since Otter's column was expected to do most of its travelling by steamer, it had almost no mounted men. Only half of Herchmer's men had horses and Otter was allowed to hire six additional civilian scouts.

On April 11th, the Colonel received new orders: ". . . to get to Battleford as quick as possible." If steamers were available within two days,

Militiamen escorting an ox-train. Like other column commanders, Otter was seriously hampered by transportation problems. Ordered to move rapidly, he finally loaded men as well as supplies in waggons.

he was to take them as far as Clarke's Crossing and then to march overland to Battleford "using great caution especially on the right flank."[2]

Two days later, the force marched out of Swift Current and by the afternoon of the following day, it had covered the thirty miles to Saskatchewan Landing. There, in obedience to orders, Otter halted to wait for the steamers to appear. Caught by miserably cold weather, the troops grumbled noisily at the delay. A powerful wind across the river persuaded Captain Sheets of the *Northcote* that even ferrying would be impossible and it was not until the 17th that he could be persuaded to begin transfering the force to the northern bank of the stream. The short march to Saskatchewan Landing had persuaded Otter that the mobility of his column would have to be improved and he hastily assembled a train of two hundred waggons. This was enough to carry most of the infantry as well as food and other supplies for the march, an arrangement which would help Otter overcome the delays on the river bank. General Laurie was left complaining that his own work had been seriously hampered by this diversion of transport.

By the afternoon of the 18th, the ferrying had been completed and the march resumed. Rich and unsettled country stretched north of the river and, by using his waggons to rest the tired infantry, Otter could move fast. A small detachment raced ahead to build a rough bridge over the Eagle River and, thereafter, he moved more cautiously; Indian country, the Eagle Hills, lay ahead and Otter took all the textbook precautions against ambush. By the afternoon of April 23rd, having covered 160 miles in five and a half days, the column came almost within sight of its destination. At 4 p.m., Otter gave the order to halt and camp for the night. So far he had encountered no enemy; but Indian scouts had been

Colonel Otter and Superintendent Herchmer outside Battleford. A watercolour by Captain R. W. Rutherford, an officer in Otter's column, depicts the copybook layout of a camp in enemy territory.

spotted and the approach of the column was obviously no secret. The last few miles into Battleford passed through dense bush. If the Indians were ever going to attack him they would do so as his men stumbled through the poplar woods in the lengthening shadows of twilight. It would be foolhardly to take the risk. Instead, Charles Ross, his chief scout, went forward alone to spy out the situation. That night, from their camp, the troops could see the glow of fires on the horizon for, in a last, climatic act of defiance, the Indians had pillaged and burned Judge Rouleau's house. Otter's scouts and a few police, quickly roused, failed to intercept the raiders. Next day the column marched into Battleford and the so-called siege, which had so preoccupied the sensational press of eastern Canada, was over. The news arrived in the East at about the same time as the much less reassuring accounts of Middleton's engagement at Fish Creek.

Otter's orders had been only to go to Battleford. The uneventful march was a confirmation to Middleton that he had been misled about the allegedly desperate plight of the surrounded settlers. Panicky messages from people like Inspector Morris, he complained to Caron, had deprived him of the men he now needed to surround Riel.

Otter and his men also felt deprived—of the chance to fight. They had not come all the way from Toronto to take the place of Inspector Morris in a beleaguered Battleford. Throughout the North-West campaign, the moods of commanders and troops alternated between extremes of bravado and timidity. Having completed their march to Battleford with barely a sight of the enemy, the troops had gained great confidence in themselves, and Otter undoubtedly felt chagrin that his caution on the night of April 23rd had denied him a clash with the Indians. The sight of the devastated settlement seemed to demand revenge. The settlers, now belligerent and self-confident after their release from three weeks of confinement, made haste to explain that the Indians were shiftless and ungrateful for the bounty the government had showered on them. In such an atmosphere, it was highly unlikely that Otter and his men would be content to remain quietly in Battleford until Middleton appeared.

On Sunday, April 26th, while his men were busy entrenching the old Government House and improving their camp, Colonel Otter considered a new plan. Surely it was part of the job of relieving Battleford to give the Indians a practical demonstration of the power of the government? "I would propose taking part of my force at once to punish Pound-maker,"[3] he telegraphed Dewdney at Regina. A similar message made its way to Middleton, now waiting at Fish Creek. The General cautiously rejected the proposal: "You had better remain at Battleford until you ascertain more about Poundmaker's fort and the kind of country he is in."[4] For his part, the Lieutenant-Governor appeared delighted at Otter's aggressive intentions. "Think you cannot act too energetically or Indians will gather in large number," Dewdney replied, "Herchmer knows country to Poundmaker's reserve. Sand Hills most dangerous country to march through. Be sure to secure good reliable scouts."[5]

With Dewdney's message, Otter evidently thought that he had sufficient authority for his expedition. He assumed apparently that he was in independent command or that the Lieutenant-Governor enjoyed some precedence over General Middleton. By sending out scouts to report on the camp of the Crees and Stoneys, he could also claim that he had taken steps to acquire the additional information Middleton had asked for. In his subsequent official report, Otter explained that he had been obliged to take definite action to force Poundmaker to declare himself and to prevent any juncture with Big Bear's Crees near Fort Pitt. Such a justification says more for Otter's desperate need to rationalize his decision after the event than it does about his motivation in setting out. Lieutenant R. S. Cassels, an officer in the Queen's Own Rifles, recorded in his diary that a reconnaissance had been ordered but that it was unlikely that there would be any fighting: "The Brigadier and staff evidently think that Poundmaker would surrender if we get near him at all."[6]

For the raid, Otter picked the best and most mobile of his troops: seventy-five police, fifty of them mounted, most of the men of "B" Battery and "C" Company, twenty men from the Foot Guards detachment and

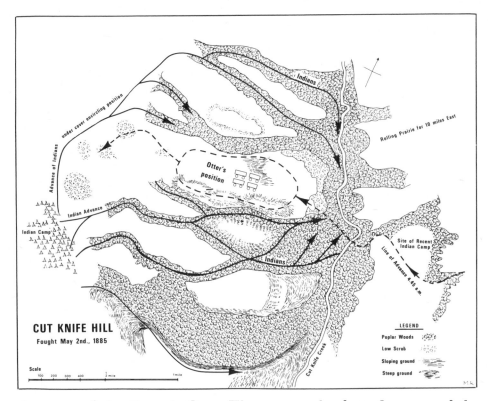

sixty men of the Queen's Own. There were also forty-five men of the Battleford Rifles, eager for revenge and, presumably, familiar with the terrain. Warned by scouts that the trail was soft, Otter ordered the "B" Battery gunners to leave their 9-pounders behind and to borrow two of the much lighter 7-pounder brass muzzle-loaders from the police. They also limbered up a Gatling gun (one of the two purchased by the government for the campaign). To carry his infantry and enough supplies for two days, Otter brought along forty-eight of his waggons. The total force, 325 men, comprised more than half of Otter's entire column.

On the afternoon of Friday, May 1st, the troops rode out of Battleford. By seven o'clock they had covered half the thirty-five miles to Poundmaker's reserve and they halted to rest until the moon rose. Then the march resumed, the scouts and mounted police in front as a screen under Herchmer's command, while the troops in their waggons jolted along behind. All night, they headed for Cut Knife Creek, a slow-moving, marshy stream where Poundmaker and his band were reportedly camped. Beyond the creek lay Cut Knife Hill, scene of a Cree victory over the Sarcees only fifteen years before.

Dawn came early, just as the first scouts rode over the hill and down the slope toward the Indian campsite. The camp had vanished. It was soon apparent that a new location had been selected more than a mile away, behind the creek and beyond a number of hills and ravines. There

Otter's approach route to Cut Knife Hill. A topographic drawing prepared for Otter's report on the battle shows the hill as the troops saw it at dawn on May 2nd.

was nothing for it but to push on across the creek, over some five hundred yards of marsh and scrub and up Cut Knife Hill, where perhaps there would be a few minutes to allow the half-frozen troops to eat their breakfast.

Poundmaker's camp seems to have been caught relatively unawares. The approach of the troops with their waggons, guns and horses, can hardly have been silent but there were few, if any, Indians on the alert and dawn was breaking before the Crees awoke to the imminence of attack. Immediately, alarm spread and the camp buzzed with activity. By the time the mounted police and scouts leading the column had come over Cut Knife Hill and down the other side, the coulees below were beginning to swarm with Cree and Stoney warriors.

Otter stopped his men where they were, deploying them to defend the top of the hill. The guns and the Gatling were pushed forward to try their fire on the Indian village. The infantry moved to the edge of the hill, to be halted by fire from the Indians below. It was Fish Creek over again, with an invisible enemy in the brush-covered coulees firing at the exposed militiamen and police on the hill above, with this difference: Otter's force would be surrounded as soon as the Indians had infiltrated the ravines which encircled his position.

With their own rifle fire ineffective the troops depended all the more on the Gatling gun and their artillery. The former, with its rattle and spray of bullets, at first alarmed the Indians but they rapidly realized that the bullets were passing harmlessly over their heads. The artillery fire was more lethal and one group of Indians dashed zig-zag fashion up the hill to try to capture the guns in a frontal assault. Police and extra gunners rushed forward to meet them with rifle fire, forcing them back.

The battle at Cut Knife Hill. In the absence of a Captain Peters, artists in eastern Canada had to portray the battle from descriptions by participants. The drawing shows the extended perimeter, the waggon corral in the centre, partially sheltered from fire, and men from the infantry school and the Battleford Rifles attempting to clear the rear.

However, fire from the guns soon slackened and stopped. Both were originally mountain guns brought west by Colonel Wolseley in 1870, and during the intervening years, their carriages had rotted with age and exposure; as early as 1881, they had been condemned as unserviceable. Now, at the crucial moment, the trail of one gun cracked and gave way. Then the other broke from its trunnions and tumbled to the ground. After each shot, the gunners had to heave the barrel back into place on its carriage, in full sight of Indian marksmen.

By 11 a.m., Otter's situation had become serious. He saw more and more casualties being dragged into the waggon corral he had located in a shallow depression near the top of the hill. War-cries and the effectiveness of Indian fire were enough to shake more experienced soldiers than lined the edge of the hill. A number of rushes from the bottom of the coulees had been repelled but it was apparent from the shouts and firing that the Indians were working their way around his rear to cut his line of retreat across Cut Knife Creek. The artillery had broken down. Indian strength seemed far greater than had been reported. Perhaps Poundmaker had already been joined by Big Bear and, instead of two hundred fighting men, there were now more than five hundred.

While Superintendent Herchmer and Major Short of the artillery kept the troops on the forward slope steady, Otter's chief scout, Charley Ross, led and cajoled men from the police, the Queen's Own and the Battleford Rifles to clear the Indians from the immediate rear. Ross went everywhere that encouragement seemed to be needed. However, Otter could not be certain that his line of retreat could be kept clear. As for going forward, across ravines where the enemy was undoubtedly concentrated, that could not be considered. Heavy with the sense that the second battle of his career had also been a defeat and that, this time, he could not escape personal responsibility, Otter gave the order to withdraw.

The two broken guns were lashed together with splints, ropes and spare harness, and hitched to their limbers; the dead and wounded were loaded in waggons and the retreat began. Sending his scouts, the Battleford men and the permanent artillery back across the creek to hold the opposite slope, Otter managed to secure a base for the withdrawal. Next came the waggons, with one of the teamsters being shot dead as he struggled to drive his team across the swampy creek bed. Finally came the rest of the troops, firing as they went, dropping back by alternate ranks.

It took the Indians some time to realize that their quarry had determined to escape and their dispersed tactics made effective counter moves difficult. It was another story once the rearguard had fallen back across the creek and the column made ready to head back to Battleford. The Indians surprisingly failed to pursue. Otter acknowledged later: "had they done so, much delay and loss of life might have been entailed upon us, as the country was favourable to them." The salvation of the retreating troops ironically enough, seems to have been entirely due to Poundmaker. Otter's dawn attack had finally committed the elderly chief to the rebellion and all morning he had been in command of the defence of his camp. However, once the troops were clearly prepared to withdraw, the elderly chief forbade his followers to continue the battle. His would only be a fight in self-defence.[7]

The newspapers made what they could of the battle, praising the steadiness of the Canadians, echoing claims of enormous casualties among the Indians and boasting that Otter had achieved his purpose of a "reconnaissance in force." Those responsible knew otherwise. On the very day that Otter had set out, General Middleton had telegraphed a warning: "Fighting these men entails heavy responsibility. Six men judiciously

A bridge constructed over the Battle River. To keep his men occupied in Battleford, Otter arranged for them to rebuild a bridge linking the two parts of the little town.

placed would shoot down half your force. Had better for the present content yourself with holding Battleford and patrolling about the country."[8] This was virtually a direct order not to proceed and, although Otter had probably not received it by the time he set out, it made it much more difficult to explain his expensive failure. Although—on no basis at all—he claimed to have killed 30-50 Indians, his own losses were definitely eight men killed and fourteen wounded. One of the dead had been abandoned on the field.

It was three days after the battle that Middleton received the first explicit news that Otter intended to march. "This is contrary to my orders to him," he wired Caron in Ottawa, "I am uneasy; he is as inexperienced as his troops."[9] Although the General's worst fears had not been borne out at Cut Knife Hill—for, largely thanks to Poundmaker, Otter had escaped the annihilation or capture which might conceivably have been his fate—neither was the engagement even remotely a success. "Am sorry Otter attacked, particularly as he retired so far and so rapidly. Doubtful of effect on other Indians,"[10] Middleton commented to the Minister.

Back at Battleford, Otter found it necessary to provide further reassurance for the inhabitants. He cautiously spread out his troops to guarantee protection for those settlers who could be persuaded to return to their homes. Small scouting parties continued to keep an eye on Poundmaker until one was surprised by Indians and fled, leaving one of its number, a halfbreed, to be killed. As Middleton had suspected, the Crees were far from cowed by their battle with the troops. Lighting prairie fires to help conceal his movements, Poundmaker began to move slowly toward Batoche, the one step which Otter's attack had been supposed to prevent. Making a wide sweep southward to avoid the white settlement, on the morning of May 14th, his scouts surprised a supply train from

A waggon train corralled in case of attack. To keep his limited forces from being spread across the prairies, Middleton ordered that supply trains would proceed without escorts, providing their own security.

Swift Current. Without resistance, the twenty-three waggons, laden with forage and special comforts for the troops from the ladies of Toronto, as well as most of the teamsters, fell into Poundmaker's hands. A few hours later, the Indians encountered a reconnaissance party of police and scouts from Battleford. One of the group was wounded in the skirmish while a policeman, thrown from his horse, was left behind to fight and die alone.

The capture of the waggons coincided with the surrender of Riel. That and the rout of the police patrol constituted the last act of rebellion by Poundmaker's Crees. Six days later, the chief sent Father Cochin, an Oblate missionary, and three other prisoners in the Cree camp, together with all the captured teamsters, to Battleford to seek terms of peace.

VI. Frenchman's Butte

At Calgary, in the heart of the Blackfoot country, settlers greeted the news of the outbreak of the rebellion with special alarm. For a long time the local ranchers had regarded their Indian neighbours with unmixed hostility and this bitterness, fully reciprocated by the Indians, had played its part in the friction with the Blackfoot during the previous summer. Moreover, wild west legends to the contrary, the ranchers and cowboys of Alberta were almost entirely unarmed. There was no militia organization and the N.W.M.P. had been greatly reduced to meet the demand for reinforcements elsewhere. Early in March, Dewdney had taken advantage of a dispute between the police and the Calgary town council over the enforcement of liquor regulations to withdraw almost all the members of the local detachment. The councillors responded by appointing their own chief of police but not until the emergency broke a few weeks later did they provide him with a weapon. And, even then, the ammunition issued did not fit his revolver.

By the Sunday after Duck Lake, Calgary, in a state of near-panic, buzzed with rumours that the Indians were already marching on the town. John Cottingham, a local businessman, reported to the Minister of Militia that complete confusion had prevailed. "I am ashamed to admit," he added, "nevertheless it is true that some of our leading citizens were much the worse for liquor, Sunday night, those whom we looked to for advice and had the Indian scare been real there would have been serious work done. I am familiar with the doings of the Mayor, Council and a few more of Calgary's drunken beauties; they glory in telling news to the public given them in confidence by Father Lacombe; in asking Comptroller White for power to Barricade the Barracks by building bastions and a thousand more foolish and unnecessary requests, while we the sober and better class are trying to do our duty in a quiet orderly way."[1]

At Gleichen, not far from Calgary, were the 70,000 acres of the Military Colonization Ranch. There, retired Major-General Thomas Bland Strange, former commander of "B" Battery at Quebec, had planned to live out his remaining years raising remounts for the British army. Like his fellow ranchers, Strange numbered the Blackfoot, like bitter winters, government officiousness and the lack of capital, high on the list of the trials of Alberta life. Among his innumerable grievances against the police and government was what he regarded as their incorrigible softness in dealing with the Indians. Drawing on a lifetime of experience, ranging from the Indian Mutiny to street battles against strikers in Quebec, Strange concluded: "With all savages, leniency has no meaning but cowardice."[2]

Strange's nickname among his fellow soldiers had been "Gunner Jingo" and he looked forward to the impending conflict as a way of settling scores with his enemies, not all of whom were Indian. Long before, he had served with Middleton; through his connections with Quebec society, Caron knew him well. With the advent of trouble, Strange moved his wife and family to Calgary and set out to organize a force to protect his property. To his furious indignation, he discovered that the Mayor of Calgary had forbidden any recruiting which might take able-bodied men from the district. He also discovered the acute shortage of arms and ammunition. On April 10th, having been notified by Middleton that he was to take charge of the Alberta district, he reported to Governor Dewdney that he had been sent no soldiers and only fifty long Snider rifles, useless for men on horseback. "It is in my opinion necessary to proclaim martial law in this district,"[3] he informed the Lieutenant-Governor.

In placing the erratic old veteran in charge of Alberta, Middleton had not been moved by great confidence in his new subordinate. Strange, he commented to the Duke of Cambridge, was "a little odd, and does funny things."[4] Nevertheless, he found in the appointment one way to quieten the appeals for help from the area and an excuse to dispose of some of the troops he regarded as less than reliable. "I sent both French regiments to the front knowing you wished it," Middleton later explained to the Minister, "but I sent them west as I did not think it wise to bring them where so many French half-breeds were to be met about here . . . ."[5] Ouimet's 65th Rifles reached Calgary on April 12th, the first militiamen from the East to reach Alberta.

For all his eccentricity, Strange was probably the most appropriate available commander for the French-Canadians in the North-West. Unlike most Canadian officers, Strange had spoken French even before he came to the country and he had carefully insisted that at least half the men in his artillery battery be French-Canadians. He was delighted to have the 65th under his command but, seeing that most of the men in

Major General Thomas Bland Strange. The former commandant of the Canadian permanent artillery school at Quebec was an eccentric individualist, an admirer of French Canadians but utterly disdainful of the Indians whose land he occupied.

Officers of the 65th Battalion en route to the West. Reluctant to use the French-Canadian battalions against the Métis, Middleton was happy to send them on to Strange.

the ranks were raw recruits, he set the battalion to a rigorous programme of drill.

It was soon apparent to government officials that the Blackfoot intended to take no part in the rebellion; indeed, if anything could provoke them to revolt, it would be General Strange with his threats, denunciations and apparent determination to deploy his trigger-happy troops for the defence of the Military Colonization Ranch. Strange, therefore, received orders to march to Edmonton, where settlers from the surrounding districts had rushed to find refuge.

It proved much harder for Strange than for the other column commanders to get a force organized. Everything, including many of his actual troops, had to be improvised from local resources; even his staff officers had to be found on the spot. There were a number of former British officers in the Calgary area, but at least some of them would not have been trying to settle in the North-West had they not suffered from some peculiarity of character or personality. Apart from Strange himself, the only officer he could find who had actually seen active service was a retired veteran of the Madras Fusiliers whom he appointed brigade major, though "his thoroughly old-time British officer manner of damning Militiamen in general and Frenchmen in particular was productive of a good deal of frictional electricity which required all my best French and most oleaginous manner to neutralize."[6]

Crowfoot, chief of the Blackfeet. As leader of the most warlike Indians in the Canadian West, he played a critical role in 1885. His choice of neutrality was of decisive benefit to the government.

With local settlers and businessmen doubling as supply officers and quartermasters, suspicions of corruption, improper influence and incompetence were even more acute than elsewhere. Strange's own autocratic manner did not make his task easier. Admittedly, difficulties to try any man's temper did exist. Rifles, ammunition and saddlery took weeks to arrive from Winnipeg and when the saddles appeared, he found them so rotten with age as to be useless. Inspector Sam Steele, expected to organize the scouts, was detained in the Rockies where C.P.R. workers had gone on strike for their long overdue pay. Some of Strange's troops had to be detached to Gleichen where the C.P.R. staff refused to work without a military escort. A party of Indians attempted to run off some of Strange's own horses and one of them was shot by the General's stable-hands.

By the middle of April, Strange's column at last began to take shape. Steele finally arrived from the mountains and began to organize a force of mounted men around the nucleus of his own small detachment of police. From Fort McLeod, Inspector A. B. Perry and another little police detachment brought up a cannon. On April 17th, Lieutenant-Colonel Osborne Smith arrived with the 91st Winnipeg Light Infantry, a battalion he had specially organized for the campaign. Smith's arrival guaranteed enough troops to overawe the local Indians and, on April 20th, Strange could at last set out for Edmonton. He left Osborne Smith in command at Calgary with orders that the Blackfoot be strictly confined to their reserves and no nonsense was to be allowed—instructions Osborne Smith prudently referred to Dewdney for confirmation.

The elderly General's orders infuriated the Lieutenant-Governor, struggling desperately to keep the Indians quiet and contented. Nor did he welcome a report from C. E. Denny that Strange had authorized sentries to shoot on sight any Indian seen running off horses. "This should be cancelled," Denny urged, "as it places the safety of the country in the hands of a few cowboys, who would shoot an Indian on sight, without waiting to see if he was running off horses or not."[7] "If military take upon themselves management of our Indians," Dewdney warned in reply, "I shall withdraw Indian Agents and all Indian Department officials."[8] At Dewdney's request, the Minister of Militia himself intervened, firmly ordering Strange to deal with the native people only through the government-appointed agents. "Afraid Strange will cause trouble," Middleton noted, adding in a private letter to Caron, "I always thought it a dangerous experiment giving him command. He is a good

fellow but he is what you call in this country a 'crank' and with a little religion in it which is dangerous."[9]

For all his strong feelings about keeping watch on the Blackfoot Indians and protecting his own property, Strange was also under pressure to pursue the perpetrators of the massacre at Frog Lake and to relieve the frightened settlers in northern Alberta. As with General Middleton, transport turned out to be his greatest difficuly. To carry all that the force would need required 175 waggons and carts, and even that would be sufficient for only a part of his force. His first contingent amounted to scarcely more than a baggage guard for a column that stretched as much as two miles in length. It consisted of twenty policemen and forty scouts under Steele and Strange's ranch foreman, Major George Hatton, with 160 men of the 65th Rifles under Lieutenant Colonel Georges-A. Hughes. The commanding officer of the battalion, Colonel Ouimet, seems to have been unnerved by his situation. After urging that Bishop Grandin at St. Albert should be approached to negotiate a safe conduct for the column and having been rebuffed by Strange, Ouimet returned to Winnipeg,

Men of the 65th help pull Strange's gun through the muskeg. Half-forgotten in the attention lavished on the other columns, men in Strange's force struggled through some of the worst marches of the campaign.

apparently to arrange to have the baggage for his battalion forwarded. Then, for the sake of his failing health, he continued on to Montreal. Strange was perhaps content to see Ouimet disappear. Hughes, a brigade major on the militia staff and future Montreal police chief, was a much tougher and more experienced campaigner.

The march from Calgary to Edmonton, 208 miles long, proved as rigorous as any of the other long treks during the campaign. The spring thaw had broken up the trail and many stretches had been reduced to a quagmire, "through which the waggons had in some cases even to be dragged by the men, the horses finding no footing . . ." The most miserable work fell to the lot of the infantrymen of the 65th. At times, the men would be up to their knees in the thick black mud, tugging the waggons through the soft places on the trail, at others, they would have to run to keep up. At night, they had to stand guard around the big waggon train.

Inspector Perry, the rest of the 65th and the gun followed three days behind. When Perry reached the Red Deer River, which Strange had forded with difficulty, he found that it was in full flood. It took the French-Canadians, many of them skilled woodsmen, only two hours to build a raft strong enough to take the gun but actually crossing the stream was another matter. The rope holding the makeshift craft broke and the ferry and its cargo and crew were carried several miles downstream before fetching up against a steep part of the bank. Then the cannon, carriage and ammunition had to be hauled up thirty feet to the bank, to be dragged back to the trail. Another two days were spent in constructing a more satisfactory craft.

Strange's advance party reached Edmonton on May 1st, with Perry and his men arriving on the 5th. The General praised his French-speaking soldiers for their endurance and high spirits and for their talent in building bridges and improving roads. He could afford to overlook the antagonisms which had developed during the march between soldiers and the teamsters, civilians under contract to the government. The inevitable conflict between those who ride and those who walk had become accentuated by differences in language. At one point during Perry's march, a sergeant accidentally dropped his rifle under a waggon. The driver, trying to force his team up a steep slope, refused to stop. Instead, he aimed a stream of curses and a blow from his whip at the offending soldier. Immediately, furious men of the 65th surrounded him. Only Perry's intervention prevented violence. That night, the teamster was dismissed and his wages were confiscated to pay for the damaged rifle.

Strange had sent orders ahead to Edmonton to build flat boats for his passage down the North Saskatchewan. While this work was being completed, he busied himself with training his raw troops, reorganizing his transport and dispersing half the companies of the 65th to garrison local settlements and key points along his route to Calgary. Next, Strange

Troops on a barge on the North Saskatchewan. While half of Strange's column marched along the shore, the rest poled their way along in leaky, makeshift barges.

sent the remainder of the 65th, together with Steele's scouts, east along the river to Victoria. Like other commanders during the campaign, he had trouble with his civilian transport workers. His teamsters now refused to leave Edmonton until they received arms for their own protection, compelling Strange to promise them rifles as soon as they reached Victoria. It was also difficult to get boatmen for his newly built barges. "I was obliged to discharge the first set hired," he reported, "they allowed the boats to sink for want of bailing." Halfbreeds, he found, were the only competent men for the work and, not surprisingly, they were reluctant to volunteer.

On May 10th, Colonel Osborne Smith arrived with the Winnipeg battalion. He had handed over the defence of southern Alberta to Lieutenant-Colonel Amyot and the 9th Voltigeurs. For some weeks, the Quebec militiamen had been on the sidelines in Winnipeg, an exasperating place to be stationed. A number of men fell sick from the cold and damp at the campsite and the townspeople began to comment on the suspect loyalties of the French-Canadians. Amyot intervened directly with the Minister of Militia to have his unit sent farther west. "I think I can manage it,"[12] Caron replied, "if you keep quiet and not let out that I am interfering." Within forty-eight hours, orders had come. As the 9th proceeded westward along the C.P.R., Caron received frequent reports and advice from the colonel-politician. He found General Laurie, at Swift Current, "a perfect soldier" but Middleton was accused of excessive haste, "consequence being immense useless expense." Americans, Indians and halfbreeds should be used for the fighting, Amyot observed, since Middleton's men were "exposed to be slaughtered."[13]

The 9th Voltigeurs reached Calgary on April 29th. It may not have been the best place for so nervous and critical a man as Amyot. Within a week of his arrival, Caron had been informed by urgent telegrams that Strange antagonized the Indians by refusing to shake hands with them, that the local supply officer was a self-confessed incompetent; and that the 9th had been broken up into small garrisons to allow Osborne Smith's Winnipeggers to go north. "Our Volunteers are being slaughtered,"[14] Amyot reported in a further telegram. On May 17th, several days after Métis resistance had been broken by the fall of Batoche, Amyot reported an imminent uprising around Calgary which he would be helpless to control. He needed more troops, scouts, ammunition and artillery but was "fatally condemned to inaction, absurd, danger, useless to country." This time, Caron simply referred Amyot's appeals to Middleton and the General, annoyed, with some reason, that a subordinate should be communicating with Ottawa behind his back, passed on a blunt reprimand to the errant colonel. "These telegrams were essentially private, in cypher," Amyot later explained, "sent to comply with the Minister's

Guarding oats. The later battalions arriving from the east found themselves, like the 9th Battalion, assigned to guard duty at supply depots and prairie settlements far from the scene of action.

Section of Pork & flour-clad Gun-boat

Section of Hay-clad Horse-boat

In his memoirs, Strange left his own description of his attempt to build a "navy" on the North Saskatchewan.

request that I should keep him posted on my views about the campaign."[15] Amyot's anxieties were only partly communicated to his men. For them life passed in a monotonous series of guards and drills. Georges Beauregard, one of a tiny detachment stationed at Crowfoot, found that he had nothing to do but stand guard for two hours a day. He was even spared kitchen duties since the detachment took its meals in Mrs. Sullivan's boarding house.

While Amyot and his men assumed their garrison duties around Calgary, the unfortunate Colonel Ouimet was on his way back from the east. As more and more English-speaking Canadians used the outbreak in the North-West to vent their antagonism against French Canada, the performance of the two French-Canadians battalions attracted increasingly wide and critical attention. The Toronto *News* was prominent among the accusers, alleging drunkenness and indiscipline in the 65th during the journey west and again at Calgary. Colonel Ouimet's apparent abandonment of his battalion was sufficient confirmation of the charges, particularly in the abusive columns of the *News*. Neither the colonel nor his fellow Montrealer, Major Dugas, were in good physical condition but political pressure forced them back to duty. On Ouimet's return, Strange placed him in command at Edmonton.

Strange's problems were by no means limited to his French-Canadian subordinates. No sooner had Colonel Osborne Smith settled himself in Edmonton than he had lodged a formal protest against the safety of the flat boats Strange planned to use for the next stage of his advance. He went on to demand that a board of officers determine the protection afforded by the flour sacks, which were all that would stand between the troops in the barges and enemy bullets. Finally, he insisted that much of the ammunition issued to the troops should be condemned as worthless. Strange, bedevilled by so many difficulties, indignantly decried such complaints. As he later recalled in his memoirs: "The protest against the boats was met by ordering a board to assemble and take evidence of

Big Bear. As the Indian who had held out longest against the reserve system, his band had attracted dozens of like-minded men, the most bitterly resentful of conditions they associated with the coming of the white man.

experienced H. B. Co. navigators and boat builders; the penetration of flour sacks was relegated to hostile bullets, and the objectors to the quality of the ammunition advised to retain their fire for short ranges."[16]

Finally, on May 14th, Strange felt ready to move from Edmonton. Scouts in canoes led his advance, followed by five barges carrying the Winnipeg Light Infantry and the single cannon. In addition, he towed along a small ferry to allow the land-based portion of his force to cross from one side of the river to the other if necessary. It remained cold in northern Alberta in May and, on the 15th, snow fell. The flotilla moved slowly down the river, keeping in contact with the mounted troops and infantry, and not before May 25th did Strange reach Frog Lake and Fort Pitt. Gossip at Edmonton had alleged that the French-Canadians would not fight. It was a canard that Strange utterly rejected and he deliberately sent the 65th on foot in the hope that they might draw the Indians to attack. In fact, no enemy was encountered until the evening of the 27th when Steele, returning to camp, reported that he had found a strong force of Indians camped only a few miles from Fort Pitt, on the north side of the river at a place called Frenchman's Butte.

Despite his disdain for the Indians, Strange was determined, as he put it, not to "commit Custer." For all the excitement of a contact, he would proceed with caution. His force had dwindled considerably thanks to the garrisons and detachments he had left behind to guard his rear. He could only count on 197 men of the 65th and the Winnipeg battalion, 27 police and scouts and his one gun. No further supplies had been received from Edmonton and the column was now on half-rations. Loading some of his infantry in waggons and leaving the French-Canadians to follow in the boats, Strange set off immediately. It was dusk before the troops were close to the Indian position and Strange stopped to camp for the night. Since many of the men had left their coats, blankets and food behind, it was a miserable as well as a frightening wait for dawn.

After ransacking Fort Pitt, Big Bear had returned to Frog Lake. Then, on May 1st, he decided to move off to join Poundmaker. The Indians got as far as Frenchman's Butte where they decided to hold a Thirst Dance, in hope of restoring good feeling between the increasingly opposed bands of Woods and Plains Crees. Messengers, sent to Poundmaker, soon returned with the disturbing news that Battleford was alive with soldiers. Big Bear and his chiefs decided to remain where they were and the Thirst Dance continued. For weeks the Crees were apparently unaware of the movements of Strange's column; only on May 26th was

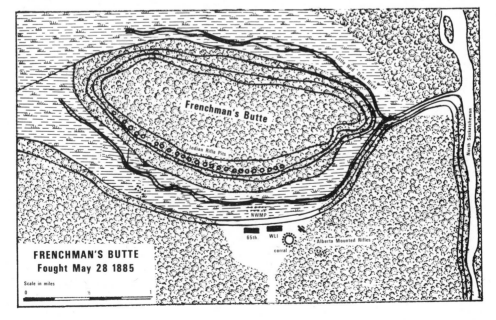

Frenchman's Butte

Indian Rifle Pits

NWMP

65th   WLI   corral   Alberta Mounted Rifles

Red Deer River

North Saskatchewan

FRENCHMAN'S BUTTE
Fought May 28 1885

Scale in miles
0   ½   1

word received that his force was approaching Fort Pitt, only twelve miles away. This caused panic in the Cree camp but not for long. Under cool leadership, the Indians hurried to take up carefully chosen positions on Frenchman's Butte, a long, conically shaped hill, crested by thick bush and facing a bare, open approach. Below the hill and on either flank, the Red Deer Creek ran through dense bush and muskeg and there was more dense bush between Strange's right and the river. It was an extremely strong position, as Strange himself could see when he came out to reconnoitre early on the morning of the 28th; the Indians' well-dug rifle pits made it even stronger.

Nonetheless, the elderly general determined to attack. The scouts led the way with the 65th and the Winnipeggers in a long, extended line behind them. The single field gun, to the rear, soon opened fire and began to register hits on the Cree position. As in the previous battles of the campaign, however the Canadians seem to have felt themselves at a disadvantage from the outset. Steele reported that the creek and swamp in front of the Butte could not be crossed by his men: in trying, one of them had already been wounded. Too short of infantry to support a direct assault, Strange ordered Steele to find a flank to turn. There was none. Steele's scouts found that the Cree position continued for a mile and

Steele's engagement with the Crees at Loon Lake. In contrast with the ponderous pursuit of later days, Steele was twice able to reach Big Bear before casualties and lack of food forced him to withdraw.

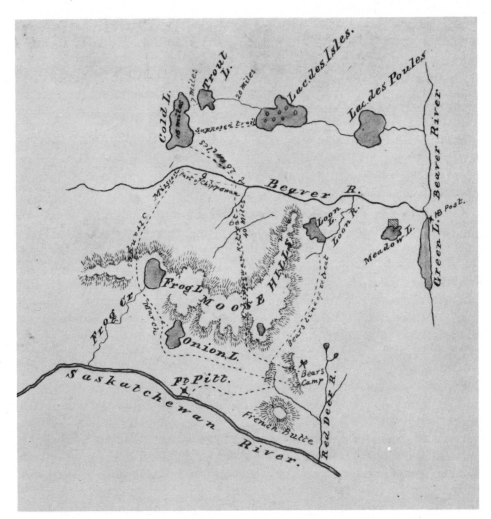

a half and that there was simply no way round. Meanwhile, on the right, where Major Hatton and a few scouts had been extended, Indians were reported circling through the woods to attack the waggons. Colonel Osborne Smith, commanding Strange's small reserve, gave his opinion that further advance was impossible, and Strange made up his mind to pull back. If, as he expected, Middleton's troops were on their way up the river from Battleford, it would be folly to spend men's lives in a needless display of bravado.

Not that retreat was necessarily any easier than advance. During the attack, two men of the 65th had been hit and Strange discovered, to his surprise, that the adjutant of the little unit did not know whether they had been collected. Finding that one of the men had, in fact, been left behind, the General was even more astonished to hear his company commander announce flatly that he would not go back for him. "General, I have been shot at quite enough today," the officer is said to have told Strange, "and I am damned if I go down there again."[17] It was left for Strange himself, with the surgeon and chaplain of the 65th, to go back for the wounded man.

By now it was raining. The Indians, as at Cut Knife Hill, failed to pursue the retreating Canadians and Strange allowed a short halt to allow his men to eat and rest. Then they resumed their march back to Fort Pitt.

During this withdrawal, in fact, the Indians had been retreating in in the opposite direction. Short of ammunition, terrified by the unfamiliar shrapnel shells bursting among them, they had fled from their positions. If the troops had known, they could have stormed over Frenchman's Butte and won the only really decisive and impressive victory of the campaign. But they had not known. The Crees, recovered from their terror, returned to their rifle pits and discovered the true state of affairs. To the despair of their white prisoners, who had hoped for an early deliverance, the Indians collected their families, their captives and most of their possessions and resumed a more orderly withdrawal. Only on June 1st, four days after the battle, did a strong party of scouts under Steele return to the site of the battle to learn that the Crees had disappeared.[18]

The next day, while men from Strange's force scrambled over the battlefield, collecting souvenirs from the goods that Big Bear's people had left behind, Steele and most of the mounted men of the column set off in pursuit of Big Bear. Within a few hours, the veteran police officer had picked up the Indians' trail: for two more days, he pushed on through the dense bush and muskeg. Twice he managed to get within reach of the Crees—on the first occasion losing one man wounded and on the second, two. By then Steele had chased Big Bear to Loon Lake, but, short of food, his horses exhausted, and encumbered by wounded men, he felt that he had gone as far as he could. At any moment, the Crees might turn and overwhelm his little force. He decided to return to Fort Pitt.[19]

By the time he arrived, General Middleton had already reached the fort by steamer to take command of the last phase of the campaign— the full pursuit of Big Bear. With that, Strange's independent command ended.

VII. Capturing Big Bear

Riel's surrender on May 15th virtually ended the North-West campaign; all else was anti-climax. One serious remaining concern, for soldiers and general public alike, was the fate of the white and half-breed prisoners with Big Bear. That white women should be captive in an Indian camp was almost salaciously appalling. Despite that, the government in Ottawa experienced a distinct sense of relief when it discovered that what had promised to be an interminable, dangerous and expensive campaign appeared to be on the verge of coming to an end.

Middleton, at Batoche, first had to dispose of his chief prisoner, Louis Riel. He sent the Métis leader to Regina, with an escort commanded by Captain George Young, of the Winnipeg Field Battery, whose father, in 1870, had pleaded in vain for the life of Thomas Scott. On May 18th, Middleton's column set off by easy stages for Prince Albert, using its two steamers as ferries at Guardepuis Crossing. On the 20th, the General entered Prince Albert, inspecting close to three hundred police and volunteers assembled by Irvine as a garrison, and pausing to receive a formal address of welcome from the inhabitants of the little town. The General had completely recovered the self-confidence he had mislaid at Fish Creek. The white settlers had been greatly surprised, he reported to Caron, "that we should have been able to drive the Indians and their wonderful half-breed fighters out of their chosen stronghold in a fair stand up fight with so little loss to ourselves."[1] As Middleton's confidence rose, so did his contempt for the police and for the unfortunate Colonel Irvine. Prince Albert, Middleton observed, had ben "hastily and imperfectly fortified at different points;" but in the circumstances it must have been apparent all along that it was "tolerably safe from attack, as the Half-Breeds and Indians are not in the habit of attacking even slightly protected positions on a level plain without cover."[2]

The attitude shared by the General and his staff rapidly communicated itself to the rank and file. To the troops, the mounted police were now "gophers," the little prairie rodents that escape from their enemies by burrowing. For their part, the police felt understandably bitter, especially when faced with the contemptuous attitude of the men from Ontario. "It is a pity these Canadian militiamen spoilt the good work they had done by never-failing bluster," wrote Corporal John Donkin, one of Irvine's men, ". . . for pure and unadulterated brag I will back the lower class Canuck against any in the world."[3]

In preparation for Middleton's arrival, Irvine had organized a mounted force of 175 men. To the Commissioner's chagrin, Middleton ignored him and his force altogether, finally announcing that the special force would stay in Prince Albert. Irvine, who felt that he had been under the General's authority from the moment that he had arrived in the Territories, also believed that he had faithfully obeyed every order he had ever received from Middleton. The General, on the other hand, was convinced that Irvine had shown neither courage nor initiative and that Prince Albert had never been in serious danger. "In point of fact, I believe that no attempt was made against it, even by Scouts, during the whole affair."[4]

Next, the General set out by steamer for Battleford, to meet Otter, the subordinate who had used his initiative with such unfortunate results. Along the North Saskatchewan, not far from the ruins of Fort Carlton, he was met by an emissary from Poundmaker, asking for peace terms. Bluntly, Middleton replied that there would be no terms. "I have men enough to destroy you and your people or, at least, to drive you away to

The steamer *Marquis* poling off a shallow. From Prince Albert, Middleton moved his troops up-river by boat. The drawing shows "grasshopper legs" being used to get the steamer back into the stream.

Indians surrendering to Lieutenant Colonel van Straubenzie. The photograph again offers a contrast to the elaborately posed illustration on the following page.

starve," and would do so, he announced, unless the Indians surrendered themselves and their prisoners without condition.[4] At Battleford he again satisfied himself that there had been no cause for alarm on the part of Inspector Morris. Only one part of the town, he reported, had ever been attacked and the other part would have been easily defensible. "The only weak spot was the Police Barracks, which was situated near a large coulee and was also hastily and imperfectly fortified, and where all the inhabitants were collected."[5] But, once again, the fort had never been attacked.

Otter's men, already demoralized by the failure at Cut Knife Hill and the renewed blockade of Battleford, to say nothing of weeks of putting up with their commander's rigid discipline, absorbed fresh blows to their self-esteem. The victors of Batoche now sneered that the famous march from Swift Current had actually been done in waggons. No wonder that Colonel Grasett of the 10th Royals found that the troops in Battleford were "down in their boots."[6]

On May 26th, Poundmaker and his band came in to Battleford to submit, an occasion recorded with suitable dignity by Captain R. W. Rutherford, one of Otter's artillery officers and an accomplished oil painter. The chief, his principal councillors and other Indians accused of murders were arrested. By the 30th, Middleton was again ready to

Poundmaker surrenders to General Middleton. The painting, by Captain Rutherford, records as many as possible of the military faces, in the best tradition of commercial art.

move on but Colonel Otter and his men, to their bitter disppointment, remained behind in Battleford.

The news of Strange's unsuccessful engagement at Frenchman's Butte had caused the General to move again. Having accepted Poundmaker's surrender, he was now convinced that Big Bear would offer as little opposition to so determined a man as himself. When one of Strange's messenger, who had lost his pistol on the way to Battleford, asked the General for another, he was apparently told: "You don't want a pistol, you could walk through the country where General Strange is with a good thick stick."[7] On June 2nd, Middleton reached Fort Pitt and rode up to inspect the scene of the battle. Characteristically, he found the Indian position not nearly so strong as Strange had claimed. There were many rifle pits but some of them were badly sited. Having sent Strange off in the direction of Beaver River to hunt for the Cree leader and his captives, Middleton set off himself on June 3rd with a force substantially larger than Strange's—225 mounted men from his various troops of scouts, 25 artillerymen with a Gatling gun, and 150 from the infantry, riding in waggons. He also ordered Colonel Otter to march north to Turtle Lake and directed Irvine to move to Green Lake. The four columns would thus form a series of barriers, east or west, for Big Bear and his followers should they try to break and run.

The pursuit could hardly be swift. Almost all the columns set out with a full paraphernalia of camp equipment, supplies and waggons, while two of them, Strange's and Otter's, were almost wholly composed of infantry. Although Steele, with only fifty mounted men, had been able to harry Big Bear effectively, Middleton started with almost four hundred

Middleton's pursuing column was able to cross the first ford at Loon Lake but was stopped by the second ford. To his critics, it seemed odd that the General was deterred when the Indians, accompanied by white women and children prisoners, had managed the crossing only a few days before.

men, horse, foot and artillery. Within a day he concluded that his waggons were too much of an impediment and he spent June 5th resting, sending back for pack saddles and having Indian-style *travois* made. He also decided, belatedly, that he could dispense with his infantry. Another day's travelling convinced him that he could manage without tents and they, too, were abandoned. It was only on the 7th that Middleton's force reached the scene of Steele's encounters with Big Bear's rearguard, a journey the smaller force had completed in less than two days. Next day Middleton's men came to Loon Lake. The entire column crossed one ford and the mounted men were able to swim their horses across a second narrow strip of water where one lake joined another, but beyond the narrows lay a broad strip of deep muskeg. After camping for the night and reflecting on his problem, Middleton decided that he had gone far enough. The muskeg was apparently impassable—he, himself, had sunk in it up to his horse's girth. Further use would make the passage even more difficult and his transport and artillery certainly could not make their way across. Evidence had reached him that the prisoners were still alive and that the Indians were apparently in desperate straits. The troops had found the body of an elderly Indian woman who, scouts claimed, had strangled herself rather than fall into their hands. By June 12th, Middleton and his men were back at Fort Pitt.

A similar lack of success dogged the other columns. Although Colonel Otter took 385 men and two cannon with him to Turtle Lake, he only had twenty-five mounted scouts, hastily organized by one of his officers.

Although they could not catch Big Bear, Middleton's column received the surrender of other Indian bands. Missionaries and officers pose beside a submissive Chippewayan chief.

It was a miserable trip for the infantry and gunners, struggling across muskeg and creeks, pulling their guns and waggons with them. As with all the other columns, they found the heat heavy and the flies intense. Only the scouts were of the slightest value in detecting Indian movements. Although it was apparent that Big Bear, or some members of his band, were in the vicinity of the Pelican Hills, it was utterly impossible for men on foot to engage in a serious pursuit. On July 1st, Otter's men finally struggled out of the wilderness, finding at least some comfort in the conclusion of their scouts that the Cree chief had broken up his band and now must be almost alone.

Strange's column did not even have the satisfaction of finding traces of Big Bear's passage, although it did receive the submission of Chippewayans, reluctant allies of Big Bear who had slipped away even before the battle at Frenchman's Butte. The route to Beaver River was, if anything, more difficult than Otter's and once again Strange had to rely on the hard-working men of the 65th to drag the one cannon through the swamps. After a few days, even Colonel Hughes was exhausted and he warned Strange that his men could go no farther. Having marched more than five hundred miles, the Montrealers, as Strange himself notes, had literally "tramped the soles off their boots." Again by his report, after he had spoken to them in French, appealing to their courage and reminding them of the white prisoners still in Indian hands, the men of the 65th responded with a cheer and somehow found the strength to push on. The only fatal casualty in the battalion throughout the campaign occurred from exhaustion on the last few days. "(T)hey have not belied the old opinion I always had of them," Strange wrote to his wife, "they have dragged our cannon through swamps and bushes, their boots are worn out. They are footsore and weary—but there was no flinch in them in the fight of which they bore the brunt."[8]

Of all the four columns sent in pursuit of Big Bear, Irvine's had the most success; it was also the most mobile. Leaving a small detachment at Fort Carlton, the N.W.M.P. Commissioner made a wide circuit to Green Lake and Pelican Lake, with scouts sent westward to Loon Lake. On June 23rd Irvine had definite word of the direction Big Bear had taken and he doubled back toward Fort Carlton, in close pursuit. On the way, he learned that the chief, accompanied only by a young boy, had surrendered to Sergeant Sharp at the fort on July 2nd.

After the brush with Steele on June 4th, the Woods and Plains Crees became increasingly divided. From the first, the former had been less than enthusiastic about defying the government while the latter felt uncomfortable in the unfamiliar bush setting and were tired of being pursued. At a conference, it was agreed that both groups should head off to join Louis Riel. Big Bear and the Plains Crees set out, striking eastward, but after following for a short distance, the Woods Crees turned north.

A few of the white prisoners had escaped in the confusion after the battle at Frenchman's Butte but the Woods Crees kept custody of the remainder, hoping to use them to win better peace terms. Thus, when McLean, the Hudson's Bay Company factor, agreed to negotiate on their behalf, the offer was gratefully accepted. With a few supplies and some fresh moccasins, McLean and the twenty-six remaining prisoners were released and directed on a 140 mile journey to Fort Pitt. Fortunately for them, they met some of Middleton's troops at Loon Lake and could travel the rest of the way in somewhat greater comfort and security.

Almost all the troops found the last phase of the campaign to be the most tiresome and difficult of all. For most, the excitement had ended. The blundering pursuit of Big Bear proved exhausting and inconclusive. Grumbling was rife. To Steele, it seemed absurd that a patch of muskeg should have stopped Middleton when he had apparently been so close to Big Bear—only a few days before it had been no insuperable obstacle to delicate women and children. "The staff, however, would not listen to any representations made by members of the Mounted Police, nor to the evidence of their own senses. . . ."[9] Men possessed with a sense of urgency about rescuing the prisoners easily became infuriated by the apparently leisurely observance of military routine. Middleton's progress through the bush was naturally contrasted with that of the unorthodox Inspector Steele. "With us everything has been done with regard for dignity and thought and the eternal fitness of things . . .," grumbled an anonymous member of the Land Surveyors' Scouts, "orders are issued at night with unfailing exactness, and the start in the morning is never more than an hour or two behind time."[10]

For most of the militiamen on the North Saskatchewan, the thrills of

The ladies of Toronto packing parcels for their men. Beyond the bare necessities provided by the Militia Department, extra food and clothing depended on the haphazard availability of private charity.

campaigning had by now rubbed very thin. Mosquitoes made their lives miserable. Months of campaigning had worn their clothes to rags. Although sun helmets and summer uniforms of Halifax tweed had been ordered, they were kept in store. Everywhere troops complained of monotonous food. "Our grub is disgraceful—hard tack and fat pork— poor tea twice a day, none at noon, with orders not to drink the water," a soldier wrote to the Opposition Leader, Edward Blake, "the authorities deserve censure for this treatment."[11] Surgeon George Sterling Ryerson stopped a hunger strike among men of the 10th Royals by administering a liberal dose of emetic but by mid-June he was beginning to find symptoms of mild scurvy among the men of his battalion.

In Eastern Canada, relief committees had been busy collecting food, underwear and other comforts for the troops but delivery of these supplies was haphazard and transport officers frequently obstructed them, demanding proper authorization for the shipments. Even when food and other "extras" reached their destination, they did not invariably improve morale. "A great deal of dissatisfaction" was recorded by Rifleman John Forin of the Queen's Own, ". . . concerning the distribution of Regimental stores which are not being dealt with proportionately: men consider that goods sent from our friends should be divided—share and share alike."[12] This democratic approach hardly fitted the military ethic or the interests of the officers. Corporal George Needler and a working party, making off with some delicacies reserved for the officers of the Queen's Own, caused a furious uproar and the entire battalion was paraded to be scolded by its commanding officer.

Many of the militiamen had other worries. After all, they were only

Welfare supplies were obstructed by government officials, delayed by lack of transport and, on one occasion, captured by Indians. When they did arrive, there were sometimes disputes about their distribution.

As in every war, most of the time was spent in waiting. That, the militiamen had not volunteered to do.

part-time soldiers: some of them had left business, most of them jobs, to come to the North-West. The excitement and the enthusiasm of March and April had worn off, giving way to more realistic concerns as the summer approached; military life had degenerated into the monotony of guard duty and drill. Caron's friend, Colonel Oswald, whose Montreal Garrison Artillery had only arrived in the West fully a month after the main body of militia, was already fed up with garrison duty at Regina: ". . . a number of us feel that this loafing is not what we came for—We are all ready and anxious to fight for our country—but . . . garrisoning a place like this is more suitable work for regularly enlisted troops."[13] The impatience of the troops was echoed at home. "Our Fall trade commences next month," a Toronto drygoods merchant informed Caron, "and if the hands are not back before the 1st August their places must be filled."[14] "It would be an outrage for men to be detailed from their professional or other profitable business avocations for a longer period than the exigencies of the public service demand," commented the *Illustrated War News*, reflecting a much wider spectrum of editorial opinion.[15]

A further factor, of which Caron must have been acutely aware, was the growing antagonism between French and English which the campaign was generating. With public attention focussed on events in the

North-West, the public appetite for news was fed almost exclusively from Middleton's entourage of newspaper correspondents. There were very few reports from Strange's hard-working but remote column and English Canadians could easily have come to the conclusion from the evidence placed before them that the French Canadians were undisciplined, the commanding officer of the 65th was a coward and the two battalions from Montreal and Quebec had been hidden in Alberta because they would not fight. In parliament, an Ontario Liberal, John Charlton, rose to stoke the fires of prejudice, claiming that six Protestants in the 65th had been punished because they had refused to take part in celebrating the feast of Corpus Christi.

Understandably, the French Canadians were acutely sensitive to such attacks, and to the slights and injustices which they believed that they had suffered during the campaign. Charles Bossé, the paymaster of the 65th, was convinced that even General Strange harboured a malignant hatred for the French Canadians. Others might sometimes claim that 'Gunner Jingo' was mad but Bossé was not fooled: "his actions contain too much venom and too much carefully planned consistency to allow anyone to think that he is mentally deranged."[16] At Calgary, Colonel Amyot had gone on collecting fresh complaints against the staff officers at Winnipeg. One of the men of the 9th had died there and Amyot claimed that Colonel Jackson had rifled the man's pockets to get money for his burial. In fact, the dead man's uncle, who lived in neighbouring Saint Boniface, had refused to allow his nephew to be buried at public expense and the local French Canadian community had raised a substantial sum for a memorial. Amyot was not placated.

The Minister of Militia was as anxious as anyone to end the campaign quickly. Even if the victory had come sooner than anyone had anticipated, it was still terribly expensive to keep an army in the field and Caron knew that he would be held personally responsible by his cabinet colleagues and his political opponents for any evident extravagance. Within two days of the fall of Batoche, Wrigley had proposed drawing on the government for the $204,000 owed the Hudson's Bay Company for supplies and transport. At the same time, however, came rumours of gross mismanagement in the transport and supply arrangements for the campaign. Some of them came from disappointed contractors and their political allies, but a report from Colonel Whitehead, the Minister's own appointee, was emphatic in its accusations. "You are surrounded by thieves," the Montreal businessman telegraphed Caron on May 24th; "Supplies have been sent forward sufficient for 20 thousand troops—the waste is ruinous. Your councillors recommended and succeeded in appointing their own employees as transport and supply officers, and rushing car loads to the front without proper requisition."[17]

Whitehead had immediately become suspicious of Major W. R. Bell,

ENOUGH TO MAKE THE GHOST OF TWEED BLUSH.

Rather unfairly, *Grip* blamed Macdonald, Dewdney and Nicholas Floyd Davin, editor of the Regina *Leader,* for the alleged profiteering of Major W. R. Bell. Boss Tweed of New York would have regarded the corruption as distinctly bush league.

the manager of the Bell Farms, whom Middleton had left as his supply and transport officer at Qu'Appelle. It was Bell who had arranged for most of the $10-a-day teaming contracts, a rate which Whitehead now condemned as grossly inflated. Moreover, even after Middleton had moved on from Clarke's Crossing and the river had been opened for navigation, Bell had continued to send loads of hay along the prohibitively expensive land route simply, he explained, because no one had told him to stop. Now the hay lay rotting and unwanted. Whitehead cancelled and renegotiated the contracts of as many teamsters as he could find but many of the teams under contract were with General Middleton, beyond his reach.

Both Wrigley and Middleton understandably found Whitehead's blanket charges of malfeasance and mismanagement and his alteration of their arrangements annoying and ill-considered. Wrigley adopted the position that his company had acted throughout only on requisitions from military officers and that the General, not Whitehead, really knew his own requirements. Certainly, Wrigley acknowledged, there were always would-be contractors who would submit lower tenders but there was no guarantee that they would deliver. For his part, Middleton had complete faith in his appointees, Bedson and Bell, and he preferred to blame any difficulties on the Hudson's Bay Company and the staff officers in Winnipeg. For Caron, it was all very confusing. On whom could he rely? Who were the officers who were at fault? Who were the "thieves?" Wrigley had claimed that he knew of more economical ways of hiring transport but government officers had failed to act. "Let me know confidentially," Caron telegraphed back to Wrigley, "if anyone is putting obstacles in way." Later, on the same day, he added: "I wish you would keep me posted as to what is going on. I look upon you as my Confidential Adviser and wish you to do all you can to ensure success of transport."[18]

When a government minister had to beg a leading contractor for secret information about the government's own operations, he was paying the price of improvisation. The makeshift staff at Winnipeg had soon cracked under the strain. For some weeks in April and May, Colonel Jackson lay sick and at no time was he able to exercise any personal supervision beyond Winnipeg. Nor was Whitehead's appointment as chief transport officer clearly defined, particularly with respect to Wrigley. And Whitehead, once he felt that he had reformed the transportation system, seems to have felt entitled to improve the supply system as well. A number of bases, scattered along the C.P.R. line, still operated without apparent supervision or coordination, each with officers hiring transport, requisitioning supplies from the Hudson's Bay Company, and acting as a law unto himself. The only real connecting link was the great trading company which provided the supplies and which earned a flat five per cent for all that it did for the government. Already the Hudson's Bay Company was sufficiently unpopular with competing local merchants to be reluctant to impose puritanical standards of profit-making on its subcontractors.

The main advanced based for the field force had been established at Swift Current under Major General Laurie but the importance of this

The station at Swift Current. As closest point on the C.P.R. line to the South Saskatchewan, it had been selected as Laurie's headquarters and the main base for supplies and hospital services.

location had gone with the opening of the river for navigation and the passing through of the Galt steamers. Its main role, thereafter, was to supply Otter's force at Battleford. Laurie was unjustly held responsible for the capture of the waggon train by men from Poundmaker's band on May 14th. In fact, it had been on Middleton's insistence that teamsters had travelled unarmed and unescorted. When news of the capture reached him, Laurie assembled a train of 150 waggons, dismissed drivers who refused to join, and stood ready to lead a second relief of Battleford in person when the news arrived that Poundmaker had surrendered.

On May 22nd, Middleton authorized the transfer of the main base eastward to Moose Jaw. The main advantage seems to have been that there would be better hospital facilities for the wounded, now being brought south from Saskatoon. The arrangements for the move illustrate the growing complexity of the campaign. A large stockpile of supplies had accumulated at Swift Current but, Laurie soon found, there were no steamers available to transport them around to Battleford. Instead, he arranged with two local teaming firms to do the work over a two-week period. No sooner was the contract arranged than Major Bell intervened with a lower tender. When the dust cleared, it turned out that Bell had acted through a dummy, that his tonnage rate was higher than the previous contractors' and that he was not committed to a time limit. It also turned out, to Laurie's indignation, that Bell got the business. It was a full month before the supplies had been moved and their militia guard could be removed.

Although he resented his obscure administrative duties and considered them, with some justice, to be beneath his dignity, Laurie got little sympathy from General Middleton. To Caron, the General complained that Laurie was "fidgety and inclined to interfere and wish I could be rid of him."[19] The old general also managed to exasperate Colonel White-

head: Laurie, he claimed, was "another 'snag' in the force," "a fifth wheel to a coach interfering in every department . . ."[20] During the campaign, Caron had done little to help Middleton get rid of staff officers like Laurie, Strange or Colonel Houghton, but now he was more prepared to oblige. When Laurie incautiously complained about being sent orders by a military subordinate, Colonel Jackson in Winnipeg, Caron replied that he assumed that he could best meet the General's wishes by relieving him from his command.

Only the ending of the campaign would give Caron respite from the stream of conflicting reports, accusations, complaints and criticisms which flowed across his desk. On June 21st, word finally came from Middleton: the last of Big Bear's prisoners had been recovered and the troops could begin to come home. "(S)hall go on reducing everything as hard as I can,"[21] the General promised. Within a few days, Caron had wired his demobilization plans. "Am anxious to get back married men, clerks and Civil Servants," the Minister explained, "Relief Committees pay for families of married men. If returned, this could cease."[22] Such a sorting was neither possible nor necessary. With the exception of the permanent troops and the two battalions of Winnipeggers specially raised for the campaign, all the troops would be coming home together. There was even a ministerial intervention to ensure that Colonel Oswald's battalion, the last to arrive, would come home as soon as the others.

By the end of the campaign, most of the Canadian troops in the North-West were on one or the other of the two main transportation axes, the North Saskatchewan river or the Canadian Pacific Railway. This enormously simplified and speeded up the task of bringing the men home. Middleton sent his steamers west to Edmonton to collect Ouimet and the scattered companies of the 65th and then they dropped back down

Convalescents at Swift Current. The number of damaged arms is testimony to the dangers of mounted warfare and, perhaps, to the fact that more serious wounds tended to be mortal.

Lieutenant Colonel Arthur Williams M.P., commanding the Midland Battalion. His death at the end of the campaign established him as a symbolic victim for all the slights allegedly heaped on Canadians by Middleton and his British staff officers.

the river, picking up militia at Fort Pitt and Battleford. Many of the men were packed in barges and towed along behind the steamers. It was slow work. Now that summer had come, water levels in the river fell rapidly and the steamers repeatedly ran aground.

Soon after leaving Fort Pitt, the force suffered its last major casualty when Lieutenant-Colonel Arthur Williams of the Midland Battalion died. He had suffered for a few days from the symptoms of typhoid fever and sun stroke but his early death was unexpected. To the Canadians with Middleton, Williams had been *their* senior officer in an organization dominated by a British general and his British friends. Popular and attractive, Williams had been an obvious focus for those who had come to resent their treatment at the hands of Middleton and his staff or who bridled at the General's evident mistrust of militia subordinates. Williams had come West partly because he had substantial investments in land in the Territories but mainly because he was eager for military experience; he had little patience with the military professionals who supposedly ran the campaign. "Save us from the 'regulars'," he had written to Caron on his way to Batoche, for they seemed to be "the only ones in whom confidence is placed. . . ."[23] Williams' death helped to confirm him among his fellow Canadians as their particular hero, the man who had stood up to Middleton, who had inspired the final, victorious charge at Batoche. Moreover, it was alleged, after that battle, Middleton had deliberately slighted and ignored him. Colonel George T. Denison, an intense nationalist, was prepared to attribute William's death to the insults and snubs he had suffered at the hands of the General and his staff officers.

While Middleton and his men proceeded down the North Saskatchewan, portaging at Grand Rapids by means of the tramway and boarding new steamers to take them to Winnipeg, other troops rode back along the C.P.R. William Van Horne, the railway's general manager, planned to inveigle the government into sending the entire force by the rail route. Already, he had offered Amyot and the men of the 9th Voltigeurs a free journey into the Rocky Mountains; he now extended the offer to all, provided the men were first brought to Calgary. This would have netted the railway a substantial amount of revenue but it would also have compelled the troops to make a long overland march in the full heat of a prairie July; they were better off in their barges.

Commercial reasons were also not totally absent from Winnipeg's desire to welcome Middleton's victorious army, and the General himself looked forward to a grand review of his troops before they dispersed to eastern Canada. Not everyone was enthusiastic. Having had his free trip to the Rockies, Colonel Amyot of the 9th was furious at the idea of being held up for what he described as " a local circus asked for by Hotelkeepers." "It is a gross political blunder," he expostulated, "useless expense, cause of demoralization for troops."[24] In fact, the review was never held. On the day before it was to occur, a steady, drenching rain began to deluge Winnipeg. Instead of a parade, the mayor sensibly arranged

The steamer *Athabaska* brings troops home from the North-West. The homeward rush of troops was assisted by all manner of conveyances, all vying for the honour and profit of government business.

for the city's taverns to remain open all night. Since the troops had officially been denied liquor throughout the campaign, a night-long festival proved to be as satisfactory to them as to the local publicans.

The troops followed many routes from Winnipeg to the east, as railway managers and steamboat operators vied fiercely for the business. Although the C.P.R. lacked the rolling stock to carry all the troops home along its now-completed main line, it did operate two large steamers on the upper lakes which could carry militiamen to Owen Sound. Other troops disembarked at Sarnia for the benefit of the Grand Trunk Railway and at Collingwood for the Northern line. By the end of July virtually all the eastern militia had reached their homes.

There were some, of course, who would not return. Among the troops, police, scouts and teamsters who had participated, forty men had died in the campaign and 119 had been wounded. Many others would bear the effects of disease and infirmity, contracted during the campaign, to their graves.

VIII. The Execution of Louis Riel

It was now a time for reception committees, parades and civic banquets. At Toronto, George Needler found that young girls had made tiny bouquets of violets which the soldiers stuck in the muzzles of their rifles. Caron, attempting to meet the charge that French Canada had not played her full part in the campaign, brought the much-travelled 9th Voltigeurs on a wide detour through Ontario. The French-Canadians landed at Owen Sound and travelled through Dundalk and Orangeville to Toronto. Everywhere, they encountered excited crowds, enthusiastic receptions and a plentiful supply of beer and oratory. Then the battalion was moved to Ottawa so that Amyot could take his parliamentary seat and his men could form a guard of honour in time for the prorogation of the session.

Grimmer matters preoccupied the West. Riel, Poundmaker, Big Bear and most of their leading supporters were prisoners of the government, locked in police cells in Regina and Battleford, though a few, like Gabriel Dumont and Imasees, the Cree who had instigated the Frog Lake massacre, were safe in the United States. A number of immediate and mundane problems had to be faced by the military authorities. What arrangements were to be made for the continuing security of the Territories? Where were the garrisons to be located? How were the innumerable bills and accounts and requisitions to be adjusted and the host of claims investigated? Could anything be done to meet the charges of waste and extravagance which now seemed to be arising in every quarter?

While he had been waiting at Fish Creek in May, Middleton had already been thinking about the future military organization of the North-West. Clearly, the Mounted Police would have to go. They had, the General advised Caron, "completely lost all prestige with whites, breeds and Indians." What he wanted in replacement was a corps of a thousand mounted infantry, khaki-clad, with carefully chosen officers

and proper arms and equipment—"no red coats, lace and long boots."
On June 23rd, the General advised his Minister that the four permanent
force units then in the North-West and a military force of a thousand
men would be a sufficient guard for the region until winter although
"there is no doubt that if the thousand mounted men are still called
Police and left under Irvine, and with same organization—people will
be uneasy . . ."[1] In June, Parliament agreed to expand the Mounted
Police to a full thousand men. Another act placed members of the force
under the Militia Act and gave the officers the equivalent of military
rank. Henceforth, inspectors would rank as lieutenants and the commissioner would be *ex officio* a militia lieutenant colonel. For the most part,
the police had remained loyal to their Commissioner and bitterly resentful of the arrogant pretensions of Middleton and his military staff. Despite their opposition, the General was determined that the force would
be brought under the Militia Department and he even approached Lord
Melgund, his former chief of staff, to become the next commissioner.
The challenge appealed to Melgund but the prospect of exposing himself and his newly-married wife to life in Regina persuaded him to
decline.

So long as the reform and expansion of the police remained to be
worked out, troops remained in the prairies. Colonel Osborne Smith's
Winnipeg battalion was at Fort Pitt while the permanent artillery and
"C" Company of the Infantry School Corps were concentrated at Battleford under Colonel Otter. During the 1885 session, Caron had obtained authority to expand the permanent force from 750 to 1000 men;

Mounted police on parade in 1888. Middleton's recommendation that the NWMP should
become a khaki-clad military force was ignored. The force was enlarged, several officers
retired, but it remained a police.

this enabled him to open an additional infantry school at London, Ontario, and a new mounted infantry school at Winnipeg. It was a little late for that. Although such a unit might have been invaluable a year earlier, the completion of the C.P.R. line meant that the value of posting permanent troops in the West was somewhat reduced. The railway made passage from the east a matter of a few days in a comfort only imagined by the men who passed around Lake Superior in the winter of 1885. Moreover, as Dewdney had discovered even before the campaign was brought to a conclusion, soldiers were ill-suited to dealing with the Indians: "They are unaccustomed to Indians and are more than likely to get us into trouble if brought in contact with them and are anxious to *do something*."[2] It was far wiser to reinforce the police.

In Ottawa the government faced two sources of political anxiety. One arose from the mismanagement and extravagance which Opposition critics would be sure to raise; the other was the ultimate fate of Louis Riel.

At least for Caron, as Minister of Militia, and for the officials of his department, the first problem loomed largest. Already one M.P., David MacMillan, who had served with the 7th Battalion from London, had made the point in the House of Commons. "Like all armies," he declared, "the expedition was followed by a lot of speculating suckers, who were determined to make all they could out of the affair.[3] The major problem of tying up the loose ends lay in the utter disorder of the accounts for the campaign. Dozens of officers had been authorized to submit requisitions and some of them had even delegated the authority to subordinates. If most of their business had been with the Hudson's Bay, it was also true that the Company's posts were widely scattered and communications were frequently poor. In Strange's Alberta column, there had been persistent confusion about who, beside the General, could sign vouchers, and with Strange hundreds of miles away in the wilderness, the question was not academic. Of course, there was also the all too conspicuous role of Major Bell as supplier and purchaser of hay and transport. His case, already widely known across the West, came to public notice through an article inspired by a disappointed rival in the major opposition newspaper in Winnipeg, the *Free Press*. The charges could hardly be ignored:

> Not a dollar short of a million, we have every reason to believe and do believe, was in effect stolen from the people of Canada by those who are intrusted by the Government with the transportation of supplies for the troops.
>
> We are not making these charges at random, we want the public to distinctly understand. We know that they are true; we can prove that they are true. We know moreover the Government is fully cognizant of the facts to which we are alluding. They have been accurately informed as to all that has transpired by their own friends. Minister of Militia Caron knows as much, probably more of this

WAITING FOR THE INVESTIGATION.

matter than we. He, and therefore the Government, knows the names of every one of the gang of robbers who infested the transport service. He knows what each one of them did. He knows who were the thieves and who were the swindlers . . .[4]

The newspaper claimed to know a good deal more than it in fact did. Caron, harried by rival claims and conflicting allegations, had very little solid knowledge of what was going on in the North-West. In addition to Colonel Whitehead, the man he had named as chief transport officer, the Minister had only one other trusted agent in the field, James H. Metcalfe, a Conservative member of the Ontario legislature, who had been given the job of auctioning government supplies and horses at the end of the campaign. He, too, tangled with Major Bell— quite physically. "He is a low blackguard," Metcalfe complained to Caron, "He struck me when I was not looking at him and when I had a package of money and a Book under my arm."[5] Metcalfe's reports gave some substance to the *Free Press* charges: "This transport business furnishes the greatest field for plunder that has met my gaze for years. It is terrible! The waste is also something enormous. The number of middle men is something terrible."[6]

During the campaign, General Middleton had done his best to protect Bell from his detractors and Caron, reluctant to appear to be meddling in the details of the campaign, had done little but expostulate. With the emergency over, the Minister now decided to refuse Commissioner Wrigley further advances on his unaudited bills. The government intended to retain a healthy balance against disallowed claims. For its part, the Company could scarcely find funds to pay its own teamsters and suppliers. Everyone would have a long wait. Vouchers, prepared in the heat of the campaign, would be examined at leisure. "I am not aware of any contract which obliged Government to pay any claim which had not been previously rendered to Department" Caron stiffly notified the Hudson's Bay Company.[7]

The Minister at first intended personally to inspect all the transport accounts, the area of greatest suspicion, but he soon found that to be unworkable. During August, he would be holidaying at Rivière du Loup and he had no wish to spend his hard-earned leisure puzzling through complicated and unfamiliar documents. He found a way out by creating a War Claims Commission, with Jackson, Whitehead and Lieutenant-Colonel W. H. Forrest as members. Jackson would be the chairman. As senior officer, it was his due and, as a Liberal, he would offer the best protection against the opposition in parliament and local interests. Whitehead had already demonstrated his value while Colonel Forrest, paymaster and superintendent of stores at Quebec, was already one of Caron's trusted political agents. "Every claim must be gone into," Caron warned Jackson, "and I trust to you to cut down without mercy. The country will stand by you and we need not be anxious about any little dissatisfaction ..." Claims would be referred back to Caron with the commission's recommendation and "have no hesitation in using the knife," the Minister reassured them.[8]

The commissioners faced a long and thankless task. If the Hudson's Bay Company was increasingly desperate for its money, so were many lesser men whose participation in the campaign had cost them a spring's sowing or the possibility of better paid employment. If the campaign had brought a welcome influx of activity to the Territories, it was still true that the region as a whole was economically stagnant and the extra money was badly needed. If Caron had hoped that Colonel Jackson would become a lightning rod for indignation among dissatisfied claimants, he was prescient. "I will say and Col. Whitehead will endorse it," wrote Major George Hatton from Calgary, "that Col. Jackson has acted in a most ungentlemanly manner not only to me but to other citizens of Calgary. It is my intention to have it out with him if it costs me ten times the amount due."[9] William Boyle, president of the Qu'Appelle Valley Farming Company and Major Bell's employer, was blunt: "Being a good Conservative & one anxious to see the 'Great Party' remain in power & returned again with an overwhelming majority I would say that a great deal of harm is being done here by all these complications over payment of claims."[10]

By the end of 1886, when the Commission's work had been wound up, Jackson found that he had processed more than 1,600 claims, most of them small. For their services in the campaign, the C.P.R. had claimed $852,431 and the Hudson's Bay Company $1,737,032. From claims totalling $4,265,564 the Minister and the Commissioners between them had

A reunion of Boulton's Scouts in 1924. Survivors of the campaign received a medal, a modest land grant and the thanks of Parliament.

cut $501,491. After prolonged investigation the Commission reluctantly recommended that Major Bell be paid $5,139, "whatever may be thought of the conduct of an officer who takes means to raise the market price of the goods which the Government is obliged to purchase."[11] The investigation found that Bell had sold the Hudson's Bay Company "a large quantity of hay at at very high price," although it did concede that he might have erred through zeal rather than through self-interest in shipping so much of it to rot at Clarke's Crossing.[12] The Commision, in its final report, acknowledged that it had probably failed to satisfy everyone "as persons who present excessive or doubtful claims are sure to be more clamorous than the honest dealer." "It cannot be denied . . .," the commissioners concluded, "the people generally in that part of the country adhered to the time-honoured practice of getting all they possibly could out of the Government". Even then, there was room for consolation: ". . . the amount so expended in the North-West Territories has gone to our own people, and will be expended mainly in improving and beautifying their homesteads and enhancing their value; and there must be a modified satisfaction in the feeling that since the money had to be expended, it has not been entirely lost but has gone to assist a new and struggling population, and to give an impetus generally to affairs in the North West."[13] The trickle-down theory of ill-gotten gains has rarely been more eloquently defended in Canada.

Dissatisfaction in the aftermath of the campaign was not limited to unpaid contractors. Returning militiamen found, like soldiers after every war, that their rewards were not proportionate to their sacrifices. In the last weeks of the 1885 parliamentary session, legislation had been adopted granting each of the volunteers 320 acres of prairie land or $80 in scrip. That, the official thanks of Parliament and their militia pay, was to be the recompense for months of service. The government had also hastily devised regulations for active service pensions. They were not overly generous. A private soldier who had been so badly disabled as to need care and assistance for the rest of his life could expect a pension of between 45c and 60c a day—without benefit of a military hospital or other additional care. A soldier's widow might expect a gratuity of a year's pay and an annual pension of half her husband's pay provided the man was killed in action or died of wounds within twelve months. If he merely died of illness directly attributable to this service, she was only entitled to 3/8ths of his pay. In any case, a widow lost her pension if she later remarried, was of wealthy circumstances or "subsequently proved unworthy of it."[14]

After considerable negotiations the troops received a campaign medal. The possibility of such a reward had been raised by Lord Lansdowne in May. The British had long since insisted that the authority of the Queen as "the Fountain of Honour throughout her Empire"[15] was not to be delegated although they did assume that Canada would pay the cost. Lansdowne persisted. The medal "would not be valued and had better not be given unless it is the gift of the Crown."[16] A Colonial Office clerk discovered that, by using an economical design, 5,000 silver medals would cost £1,500 while the same number in bronze would cost £500. The British Treasury agreed to shoulder the heavier burden. Having obtained medals at no cost, the Canadian government found that many militiamen were still discontented. Those who had actually been under fire resented the fact that nothing distinguished their valour from those who had spent most of the campaign guarding sacks of oats. The Duke of Cambridge, who had been dubious from the beginning about granting a medal for so trivial an affair, bluntly refused to approve special clasps "for small engagements during an internal rebellion."[17] After a full year of pressure, the British authorities gave way and furnished 2,250 clasps marked "Saskatchewan," again at their own expense.

If the issue of a clasp had been sufficiently important to propel the government into lengthy and repetitive correspondence, the question of rewards for senior officers proved to be an impossible problem. The government's enormous relief at the successful conclusion of the campaign had manifested itself in a gift of $20,000 to General Middleton and the suggestion that he be appointed a K.C.M.G. The British obliged and the War Office added its reward by confirming Sir Frederick in the rank of major-general in the British army. The Colonial Secretary, who had agreed to Middleton's knighthood, went on to suggest the same reward for the Minister of Militia. The Prime Minister, aware of cabinet jealousies, at first refused, but Lansdowne pressed the case: "Caron did his work well and with spirit and although he is, as you pointed out to me, a young minister, I am not sure that any of his colleagues not yet honoured with the K.C.M.G. have been brought before the public so conspicuously as he has during the past few months."[18] In August, Caron became Sir Adolphe.

Unfortunately, the British, as sole source of honours, were not so liberal about other decorations. For a campaign of such limited magnitude, the War Office considered it generous to offer no more than two or three of the lesser C.M.G.s. Inevitably, a very large number of senior militia officers felt themselves entitled by their services to such distinctions. Republican austerity was not a virtue in Canadian militia circles. The government found itself in a difficult position, since it was quite impossible to pick out two or three officers without infuriating a much larger number, and with sound political judgment, it was decided to give none at all. In turn, this placed Middleton in an embarrassing position. Traditionally, the task of a military commander is to secure rewards for his deserving subordinates. Now, although the Minister and the General had been generously recognized, there was nothing for those lower down, and the dilemma faced by the General and the government could not

SCURVY TREATMENT OF BRAVE MEN

easily be explained to the disappointed officers. Their sense of grievance was indeed heightened when the official report came out. Militia officers had eagerly awaited the publication of Middleton's despatches, expecting that their friends would be able to read fulsome accounts of gallant exploits. Instead, they found a particularly cold and official narrative. If Middleton was sparing of blame, except for the unfortunate police officers, he was not generous in giving praise. Nor was there any slight suggestion that the General had profited from the strategic competence of his Canadian subordinates; there was no indication that Canadian officers might have deterred him from withdrawing from Batoche on May 9th or that they might have arranged the successful assault three days later. George Needler expressed a common Canadian view when he suggested that Middleton's willingness to do so much himself easily passed over into "a too-obvious desire to assume the credit for everything himself."[19] Dr. Orton, who certainly felt that his tactical advice should have been mentioned, agreed: "It is thought by many who had opportunities of judging that General would have gained more honour and a more lasting reputation, had he displayed more willingness to accord a share of honours to others who merited it."[20]

Thus the publication of reports by Middleton and other senior officers of the campaign released a flood of counter-claims and recriminations. General Strange, who lobbied for a K.C.M.G., complained that part of his report had not even been printed. The strain between British and Canadian-born officers was recalled and perhaps magnified in the stream of personal memoirs which now began to appear in print, amplifying and sometimes contradicting the official version. Among nationalists, Otter's unsuccessful foray against Poundmaker's camp began to be resurrected as a Canadian victory. One anonymous Land Surveyor wrote that Otter's attack "broke Poundmaker's back and prevented him from joining Riel."[21] Even the Deputy Minister of the Militia Department, Colonel Eugene Panet, was not immune. Writing to Otter to obtain further details of the engagement, the elderly French-Canadian officer wrote: "Cut Knife in my estimation is worth ten Batoches, and it illustrates the fact that Canadians can fight their own battles without any foreign help."[22] That was nationalism with a vengeance.

Medals, awards and unpaid bills aroused a lot more passion in the aftermath of the 1885 campaign than most people have acknowledged; but such grievances tended to be engulfed in the turmoil of emotion surrounding the fate of the Métis leader. If Louis Riel had borne the most limitless malice toward the Dominion and its political leaders—and in most that he did and said it is far from evident that this was so—he could hardly have expected a fuller revenge. With Riel vanished the last wisps of that dream of the Fathers of Confederation—a new nationality built to replace the crippling duality of the old Union of 1841. The

The courthouse at Regina. Riel had written to Macdonald from his jail cell, asking for a trial before the Supreme Court of Canada. After his vindication, he would return to become premier of Manitoba.

uneasy tensions of Canadian federalism were suddenly and irreversibly exposed. Politically, the fate of Riel also turned out to be the doom of the Conservative party. This disintegration of one majority party made possible the emergence of the Liberals: ironically, Riel numbered some members of that party among his most remorseless enemies.

In May, Riel's surrender had marked the glorious climax of the campaign: by September, there were few sensible Canadian politicians who did not secretly wish that he had somehow slipped across the American border with Dumont.

From Batoche, Riel had been escorted to Regina to be lodged in the only available jail, the cells at the police barracks where the arrangements were not wholly satisfactory. In the absence of a walled-off exercise yard, the prisoner had to take his walks confined by a ball and chain. According to his jailer, Superintendent R. B. Deane of the N.W.M.P., this was less to prevent escape than to demonstrate to any potential white vigilantes that the rebel chieftain would be held securely until the law had run its course. Riel did not appear to mind. His first concern was for his wife, Marguerite, and his two small children, whom he had been obliged to abandon at Batoche. He pleaded with Deane for the chance to make a little money, perhaps by allowing photographs of his captivity to be sold, perhaps by selling the religious verses he had begun to compose in his cell. After a few weeks, at least some of his family worries were set at rest. His brother Joseph set out for Batoche and brought the family, hungry and ill, back to Saint Boniface. Thereafter Riel could concern himself more with his own prospects.

In 1870 Riel had seemed the symbol of French-Canadian aspirations in the North-West but, after thirteen years, his memory had been dimmed, His return to the Saskatchewan in 1884, like the grievances of Indians, Métis and white settlers alike, was equally ignored in both French and English Canada until the outbreak of the rebellion. With that, the memories and then the sympathies of nationalists were aroused. In April, at the behest of its Liberal opposition, the Quebec Legislature debated a motion blaming the events in the North-West on the federal Conservatives. There was less political calculation (but, still, a vast preponderance of Liberals) in the formation of a Riel Defence Committee under the presidency of L. O. David. The committee raised money to brief a powerful team of lawyers for the defence: F. X. Lemieux, a distinguished criminal lawyer and a future Chief Justice of the province; Charles Fitzpatrick, a partner in Caron's law firm and a future Chief Justice of the Supreme Court; and J. N. Greenshields of Winnipeg.

Riel, now penniless, was grateful for any such help but he also sensed that he was being made the pawn of partisan manoeuvring. In a letter to Sir John A. Macdonald, which illustrated his mixture of common sense and fantasy, his primary request was for a great state trial before the Supreme Court of Canada where his entire political career from 1869 to 1885 could be reviewed. Its outcome, he assured the Prime Minister, would not only be vindication for himself but exposure of the entirely hypocritical role of the Ontario wing of the Liberal Party in all its deal-

Riel's jury. Tradition to the contrary, the six men were not all committed enemies of the Métis leader and their recommendation of mercy was an embarrassment to a government which wanted an uncomplicated verdict.

ings with the North-West. However, to ensure that the party of Blake and Mackenzie met its fate, he needed a more balanced team of lawyers —at least a French-and an Irish-Conservative—and an English Protestant as well, provided he could speak French. After the trial, Riel suggested, he planned to re-enter Manitoba politics and, at no very distant date, to become premier. Then he would be grateful if Macdonald would send him Superintendent Deane as his lieutenant-governor, for no man better understood his thoughts.

These proposals, like Riel's poetry, were regarded only as amusing by Dewdney and Macdonald and, after eight weeks at Regina, Riel was finally brought to trial on July 20th. The case was heard in the drab little Regina courthouse, before Magistrate Hugh Richardson and a jury of six white Protestant settlers. The charge, read in all its archaic splendour, was treason; that Riel "not regarding the duty of his allegiance nor having the fear of God in his heart, but being moved and seduced by the devil as a false traitor against our said Lady the Queen, and wholly withdrawing the allegiance, fidelity and obedience which he should and of right ought to bear towards our said Lady the Queen ... most wickedly, maliciously and traitorously did levy and make war against our said Lady the Queen . . ."[23] The defence promptly launched a spirited legal assault of the competence of the court, claiming that a magistrate and six-man jury could not try such a serious case. That failing, the defence next demanded that witnesses, some of them Métis fugitives in the United States, be brought to give testimony. Their only achievement was an eight day adjournment, time to summon doctors who could testify to Riel's mental state.

When the trial resumed on July 28th, Riel was in better spirits. William Jackson, the educated young man from Prince Albert who had attached himself to Riel, had been tried and, without much demur from the Crown had been found insane. That was not a fate Riel wished to share but it did suggest that the government was not bloodthirsty. However, as Riel was soon to discover, the motive for the government's leniency to lesser fry was to demonstrate that one man had been the unique inspiration for the trouble. The lawyers for the Crown were as distinguished as those on the side of the defence: Christopher Robinson, B. B. Osler, Tom Chase Casgrain and D. L. Scott all followed the leadership of G. W. Burbridge, the Deputy Minister of Justice. A procession of witnesses, ranging from prisoners of Riel to his turncoat cousin, Charles Nolin, reinforced by a pile of Riel's own papers, all testified to the fact that Riel had been the central and motivating force behind the rebellion, that he had personally organized violent attacks on the police, that he had committed treason.

From the moment of their first interview with the prisoner, his defence lawyers could see only one strategy. It was quite impossible to deny

The courtroom for Riel's trial. A bearded Magistrate Richardson sits in front of the jury members, listening intently as Charles Fitzpatrick sums up the defence case: that Riel is insane. Riel, who has listened head in hands, rises to plead with urgent eloquence both his own mental balance and his people's cause. A camera records one of the most dramatic sequences in a Canadian court.

Riel's role in the rebellion and inconceivable to argue that it could be condoned: the only hope of saving their client was to prove him insane. Jackson's acquittal strengthened their determination and it became apparent in their cross-examination of Crown witnesses that Riel's sanity was to be challenged at every point. For Riel, this was intolerable. Ever since he had surrendered himself on the trail from Batoche, he had awaited the trial as the occasion on which he and his people would be publicly vindicated. He had come back from Montana to speak for the Métis: the trial, perforce, would have to be the occasion. When he struggled to interject, particularly during Charles Nolin's testimony, he was silenced by the court. So long as he had lawyers in his defence, they must be the only ones to speak on his behalf.

Although the plea must have seemed the only recourse to Riel's lawyers, even insanity may not have been a good approach. There is some evidence that the six jurymen were not the myrmidons of Orangeism they were later purported to be; as white settlers at least some of them sympathised with the grievances which Riel had tried to present as had the people of Prince Albert a year before. Moreover, for most Victorians, lunacy was a definable state of disorder. In law, it was defined in McNaghten's case whence, in Mr. Justice Maule's words: "To render a person irresponsible for a crime on account of unsoundness of mind, the unsoundness should, according to the law as it has long been understood and held, be such as rendered him incapable of knowing right from wrong." The prisoner in the dock simply did not qualify. When, to the despair of his lawyers, he was finally allowed to testify, he totally demolished the case they had sought to construct for him. It was an emotional speech, certainly disordered and rambling, but it contained the eloquent and desperate attempt of a man to prove his own sanity. Riel's words were sufficient to set the foreman of the jury weeping, according to Christopher Robinson, but they won the government's case. For their part, obviously in anguish at their part in condemning the strangely compelling figure in the dock to be hanged, the jury recommended mercy.

The recommendation proved a mere embarrassment. After a second, more ordered but passionate speech from Riel, sentence was passed. He would be hanged on September 18th. Of course, that could not be the end of the case. Riel's lawyers took their appeal to the Manitoba Supreme Court, again maintaining that the little magistrate's court in Regina was not competent to conduct the trial. Firmly rebuffed, they tried again, this time before the Judicial Committee of the Privy Council in London.

The judicial system moved much more slowly than public opinion. During the actual 1885 campaign, there had been little attempt to stir up French-English differences in Canada. The exceptions, like *Le Métis*

WHAT WILL HE DO WITH HIM?

With Macdonald torn between his Ontario Orangemen and Quebec Bleu supporters, J. W. Bengough of *Grip* could look on without much apparent sympathy for either side.

and *La Vérité* in Montreal or the *Evening News* and the *Evening Telegram* in Toronto, were on the extremes and there was little protest when the editor of the *News* was horsewhipped by a furious French-Canadian officer. Now, with the trial and the sentence, the crescendo of fury began to rise. Almost overnight, Riel became a symbol of the majority's right to impose its will and the minority's right to deny it. By September, newspapers like *Le Monde* and *La Minerve*, closely controlled organs of the Quebec Conservatives, were assuring their readers that the government would not let Riel hang. In Ontario, in the East Durham by-election to fill Arthur William's vacancy, that was precisely what the Liberals claimed in their assault on the Conservative stronghold. The Conservatives fought back hard, declaring that there could be no question that the rebel chieftain would hang. The Conservatives held the seat but the newly elected M.P. hastened to advise Macdonald of the words of one faithful supporter: "God help him next time if he don't hang Riel."[24]

To allow time for the appeal to the Judicial Committee, Macdonald twice allowed Riel a reprieve; each time there was relief in Quebec and a corresponding fury in the rest of Canada. Yet the Prime Minister never doubted his determination that Riel would die. It was not solely principle; political calculation mattered too. It seemed inconceivable that French Canada would, for long, give its allegiance to such a man as Riel, particularly when his apostasy had drawn the furious condemnation of the Church. Macdonald had a letter from Bishop Grandin himself, placing the whole blame for the rebellion on the condemned man's shoulders. His French-Canadian followers must stand firm for the storm would pass. In English Canada, on the other hand, he could detect a deep and growing emotion which must and could be satisfied, particularly as Riel was guilty. "Ontario is not going much longer to be sat on by these Frenchmen and the Priesthood," a prominent Toronto lawyer warned Macdonald, "Quiet people here are beginning to talk savagely. The Anglo-Saxons will turn some day and make them 'go halves' or drive them into the sea. The latter wd be the best place." Macdonald sent the letter to Sir Hector Langevin, a French-Canadian colleague: "The enclosed contains the views of a very violent and foolish fellow but conveys the general feeling thro the N.W., Manitoba and Ont. This must be handled with great care."[25]

Opinion in French Canada was hardly less extreme and Macdonald underestimated the fervency with which French-Canadians of all shades of opinion had identified with Riel's life and their potential depths of fury when he bluntly denied them what they wanted. Even clerical opinion was modified when Father André achieved Riel's return to the faith. Those who could not condone rebellion could not condone the execution of a lunatic either. A procession of clergy who had been exposed to Riel's idiosyncratic religious opinions and to his mysticism were utterly prepared to testify to his insanity. Finally, the whole mechanism of making the Métis leader the single sacrificial offering for a misguided but understandable rebellion struck fair-minded French-Canadians as repugnant and unjust.

In 1875, Canada had been saved from a similar impasse by the intervention of Great Britain through the Governor-General. At the time and in revenge, the prerogative powers had been sharply narrowed. Could they still be used? The Judicial Committee could not help; it dismissed Riel's appeal without even waiting to hear what the government's lawyers had to say. Macdonald, himself, deliberately discouraged any British effort to save Riel, now claiming that the rebellion was a small, insignificant affair of which the British could barely take notice. This was a subterfuge but it convinced a majority in the British cabinet. *The Times* of London reflected the bulk of official British opinion in asserting flatly that Riel, the convicted criminal and twice-rebel, must die.

Only one stop remained. To allow time for his appeals, Riel had been granted reprieves from September 18th to October 16th and again to November 10th. Once again, the government spared his life, this time to November 16th, to allow three doctors to settle, once and for all, the question of his sanity. The final reprieve, a concession to French Canada, was a hollow gift. All three of the doctors, Valade from Ottawa, Lavell from the Kingston Penitentiary and Jukes, the N.W.M.P. surgeon, found

Honoré Mercier, Liberal leader in Quebec. The violent reaction to Riel's execution made him premier of the province within two years and laid the foundation for half a century of Liberal dominance.

to a greater or lesser degree that Riel was unbalanced on the subjects of religion and politics; all were conscious of his extraordinary personal charm but none of them could claim that he was a man who did not know right from wrong or—Macdonald had generously offered the option—that he suffered from "raging dementia."

Now, only the Cabinet could save Riel. The English-speaking ministers were unanimous that Riel should die and two of the three French-Canadian ministers, Langevin and Caron, were close enough to both Macdonald and clerical opinion to be prepared to acquiesce. Joseph-Adolphe Chapleau was the critical figure, the one man in Quebec Conservatism with a broad popular following, the one man who could choose between sharing the miserable uphill fight to rebuild Conservatism in Quebec that would follow the execution, and resigning to seize the leadership of the growing popular movement on Riel's behalf. He found the latter alternative desperately appealing and Chapleau had few doubts that he could displace his old rival, the Liberal leader, Honoré Mercier. On the night of November 11th, three of Chapleau's closest friends and political confidants came up to Ottawa from Montreal. Through the night, they wrestled with the issue, trying to prepare a memorandum for Chapleau's resignation. At dawn, the friends left and Chapleau went on alone. Four hours later, they met for breakfast. Chapleau had made his decision. He would stay. As he had sat alone, he later told a friend, "Suddenly I glanced in front of me—in the distance such a sight, tumult, fighting, bloodshed, misery and prostration: and a madman looking from the window of a prison and laughing, rubbing his hands and shouting incoherent words of malediction. I was horrified." To Macdonald, he wrote later that morning: "We will have to fight, perhaps to fall. Well,

Justice not satisfied. For Bengough, the execution of Riel still left one prominent culprit unpunished.

I prefer after all to fight and to fall in the old ship and for the old flag."[26]

On November 14th it was known that Riel would die, but only on the 15th did he learn it for himself, through his confessor, Father André. He spent that night in prayer and next morning, at 8.00 a.m., they came for him. It was bright and cold as the little procession made its way upstairs and outside to the scafford in the prison yard. They were reciting the Lord's Prayer together when the trap door fell open. "Deliver us from evil . . ."

Back in Quebec, flags flew at half-mast and the merchants draped their windows in black. On the 17th the committees which had been collecting money for Riel's defence gathered to form the *Mouvement National*. Children in school encountered a new and frightening symbol of French Canada's national difference, the hangman's rope, the gibbet of Regina. Such was the price the majority paid for the fulfilment of its will.

In 1871, Blake had used Riel to win Ontario for the Liberals. Now Mercier would use him to win Quebec for the Parti National, an ill-disguised combination of Liberals and Ultramontanes. "Riel, our brother is dead," Mercier would tell the fifty thousand people packing the Champ de Mars in Montreal on November 22nd, 1885, "victim of his devotion to the cause of the Métis of whom he was the leader, victim of fanaticism and treason—of the fanaticism of Sir John and some his friends, of the treason of three of our people who sold their brother to keep their portfolios."

Mercier would win Quebec in 1886; but on the 22nd another orator also won applause. "If I had been on the banks of the Saskatchewan, I, too, would have shouldered my musket." It was to be eleven years before Wilfrid Laurier would lead his party to federal power. The Conservatives may have been losing power in Quebec; in Ontario they were busily collecting those Liberals who had been taught for generations by George Brown and the *Globe* to suspect and hate their French and Catholic neighbours. Sir John A. had a few tricks left. On March 11th, 1886, Philippe Landry, a Quebec Conservative, moved that the House of Commons express its regret that a sentence of death on Louis Riel had been carried out. Immediately, Sir Hector Langevin was on his feet to move that the question be put. One of the great debates of Canadian parliamentary history followed but the vote was inevitable and it could only be on one question: for or against the execution of Riel. When it came, seventeen French-speaking Conservatives salved their consciences but twenty-three Liberals from Ontario, including all but one of the English-speaking leaders of the party, supported the government.

The exception was Edward Blake. The Liberal leader was now convinced that the government had hanged not an innocent but an insane man and he presented his arguments in a brilliantly reasoned, if utterly boring, speech of six hours. His stand would be remembered in Ontario in the 1887 federal election. Defeated and bitter in the aftermatch, Blake resigned his leadership. His chosen successor, pulled over the heads of the chieftains of the party, happened to be the man whose eloquence had thrilled that Montreal crowd in 1885, Wilfrid Laurier.

There were other sequels. In the North-West, the execution of Riel

Prisoners, friends and captors at Regina. In front: Horse Child (Big Bear's son), Big Bear, Alexander Stewart (police chief of Hamilton, appointed by the government to present the charges at the post-rebellion trials), Poundmaker. Behind: Constable Black, Father Cochin, Inspector R. B. Deane, Father André, Beverly Robertson (interpreter).

allowed Dewdney to seek clemency for most of the remaining offenders. In all, forty-four Indians were convicted of various offences, eleven of them were condemned to die and eight were hanged. Of the Métis, eighteen were eventually sent to prison and two white prisoners were discharged. Big Bear and Poundmaker each were sentenced to three years in Stony Mountain Penitentiary in Manitoba. Poundmaker's imprisonment proved sensitive for he was the adopted son of the Blackfoot chief, Crowfoot. The Lieutenant Governor gave orders that Poundmaker's hair was not to be cut and arranged for him to send Crowfoot a telegram of reassurance. By 1887, both chiefs had been released although neither lived long to enjoy his freedom.

Among the Indians, very little in the condition of their lives changed as a result of the rebellion, for better or worse. Big Bear's band was broken up but Dewdney and the government moderated or ignored the schemes proposed by the Deputy Indian Commissioner, Hayter Reed, for subjugating the Indians to the dreary life of agriculture on the reserves. New farm instructors were appointed and the pre-rebellion policy of denying food as an incentive to work was applied with increasing severity. In some ways, though, Dewdney respected the Indians more than better-known benefactors. Asked for his advice on preventing future trouble, Father Lacombe urged the government to "consider the Indians in all respects and everywhere at least for many years as real

minors. Consequently they are not at liberty and are under the tutelage of the Government." To help ensure this tutelage, Lacombe suggested that the Indians should have their horses taken away to be replaced by cattle, as a curb on their mobility. Dewdney replied that the government had no right to take the Indians' property without their permission.[27]

At the end of hostilities, a Commission on halfbreeds moved through the Territories seeking to settle Métis land claims with grants or scrip. It was a sadly belated performance, although the Commission had actually been named before the outbreak of trouble. The government also created a Rebellion Losses Commission to compensate whites and Métis who had suffered as a result of the outbreak. Dewdney provided more direct relief to the remaining Métis at Batoche and along the South Saskatchewan as well as to people at Battleford who had lost their homes and farms. These efforts on the part of the government, together with a temporary improvement in the regional economy as a result of the completion of the C.P.R. in November, 1885, gradually restored the Territories to peace. Early in the winter of 1885-6, General Middleton

Métis leaders awaiting trial at Regina. As members of Riel's council, most were sent to prison for a year. The only two white prisoners were discharged.

made tentative plans for a "flying column" of police and militia to move across the prairies during the spring to deter possible troublemakers. All winter, garrisons of permanent artillery were maintained in enforced idleness at Battleford and in the immigrants' sheds at Qu'Appelle. However on the return of warm weather, the government, with Dewdney's concurrence, decided that the flying column would not be needed after all and that the remaining military detachments could be brought home, a year after they had left their home stations at Kingston and Quebec. After a year's experience of rumours and false alarms, Dewdney used his annual report for 1886 as a platform to denounce "Those unprincipled persons who, actuated by questionable motives, or by those undoubtedly of a degradingly selfish character, have endeavoured to circulate and keep alive rumours calculated to bring about the very condition of things which they pretended did exist and hypocritically professed to deplore."[28] They sounded like some of the same people whom Colonel Jackson encountered in settling the rebellion accounts.

Back in 1884, Frank Oliver had suggested in the Edmonton *Bulletin* that, win or lose, rebellion brought results. How far did the events of 1885 bear him out? Certainly there have been some rebellions—those of 1837 are possible candidates—in which the rebels' goals have eventually been achieved in substantial measure. It would be difficult to place 1885 in the same category. It is true that, within a year, arrangements were made for the direct representation of the Territories in Parliament. It is also true that the Half-Breed Commission settled the long and bitter question of land. However, it did so without really solving the problem

Indian leaders at Earnscliffe, Macdonald's Ottawa residence. Crowfoot and other loyal Indian leaders were rewarded with a trip to Ottawa, chaperoned by Father Lacombe (standing at the rear).

that had prevented an easy solution before, for once again a generation of Métis sold their land and moved on, some to the United States, some as far north as the Peace River country, many to drift into obscurity and certain poverty. The problem had never been to provide land but to grant it in such a manner as to achieve security of tenure and a basis for stable communities. That chance was lost and would not be regained.

The Métis were not the only people to suffer in the aftermath of the rebellion although their fate is the most tragic because it was the most lasting and the least recorded. There were other, lesser victims.

Late in the campaign, Caron had asked Middleton to bring back some souvenirs for himself, Langevin and Macdonald: "Leave it to you to select what you consider of interest."[29] It was a harmless enough request, and the General agreed to try, though he reported that it might also be difficult "as everyone in camp is trying to get souvenirs also."[30] With his other preoccupations, Middleton apparently forgot all about the request, although he did bring back a pony for Caron's children and another for his own, together with the horse that had carried him through the campaign. Unfortunately, there were other souvenirs as well.

One of the Métis who had been held prisoner by Poundmaker, Charles Bremner, returned to Battleford with a rifle that had belonged to a slain policeman. He was immediately arrested, arraigned and sent to Regina for trial. His jailers deposited his goods, the furs from a year of trapping, in the police store at Battleford. They were found there by Middleton, Hayter Reed (Dewdney's Assistant Indian Commissioner), and Bedson, the transport officer. Since Bremner had been arrested and seemed sure to be convicted, his furs seemed proper booty and packages were made up for each of the officers. The bundles were loaded on the General's steamer and there they disappeared, presumably purloined by some other souvenir hunter.

Bremner, however, escaped conviction. After his release, he soon learned the fate of his furs and headed for Winnipeg to swear out an information against the General. It was by no means easy for him to make his case but he persevered. Fortunately, it was a case the Opposition Liberals could adopt. Desperately divided on the crucial issues in the rebellion, the party could at least agree to condemn theft. In 1887, when mounting publicity forced the matter to his attention, Middleton denied everything. Public opinion was satisfied and the case was considered closed. But Bremner persisted. He went on collecting evidence and, by 1890, he had so much that the Liberals demanded a public enquiry. Before a Select Committee of the House of Commons, Middleton proved to be an evasive and unsympathetic witness. "I thought I was the ruling power up there," he told members, ". . . and that I could do pretty much as I liked as long as it was within reason." The members disagreed, condemning the confiscations as "unwarrantable and illegal."[31] In the House of Commons, Edward Blake devoted more than two hours of learned invective to the General's conduct.

Middleton, who had been making plans to retire to the presidency of a Canadian insurance company, now found his career in ruins; he would have to resign or be dismissed. Suddenly, he seemed to be friendless. In desperation, he turned to print, publishing a *Parting Address to the People of Canada* to give his version of the fur scandal and to vindicate himself from charges that he had failed to work for honours for his subordinates. He claimed, in fact, to have recommended the C.M.G. for seven of them and promotions for many more. He even gave the names.

It proved to be a gross political blunder. As shrewder men had realized years before, even seventy decorations would not have satisfied everyone. Those who had not even been recommended for promotion, like Colonel Denison, became infuriated; those who had been nominated claimed that they deserved far more. "Poor Middleton," Caron acknowledged to a staff officer, "made an awful muck of it."[32] Although his military career was now over, Middleton was not deprived of all honour. In 1896, the Queen named him Keeper of the Crown Jewels in the Tower of London, an evident rebuke to those Canadians who had driven him from the country as a thief. His Minister was less fortunate. Caron spent only a year and a half more as Minister of Militia before reluctantly becoming Postmaster General. Although he narrowly escaped

General Middleton and his family. Full of the rewards of his long career, the General looked forward to retiring to the presidency of a Canadian insurance company.

the fate of *patroneux* like Langevin, he was sufficiently notorious for the Liberals to mention him by name in their 1893 platform and for Sir Charles Tupper to drop him from the cabinet in 1896. Caron left Parliament in 1900 and died eight years later.

Other officers in the campaign had distinguished careers. Lord Melgund returned to Canada in 1898 as Lord Minto and Governor-General. Colonel Otter, whose battle had become an issue of national pride, went on to command the first Canadian contingent in the South African War at the turn of the century and to become the first Canadian-born officer to command his country's military forces. He ended his days as General Sir William Otter. Major-General Laurie turned to politics, represented Shelburne, Nova Scotia, briefly as a Conservative and then, from 1895 to 1906, the Pembroke Boroughs in the British House of Commons. Major-General Strange was less successful. In 1888, he finally left Canada, his ranch a failure, his career unmarked by title or decoration though he was, in his own view "the most distinguished Imperial officer that ever served Canada—distinguished in not having been given years ago the distinction of three or 4 letters that have fallen the lot of every officer of rank who has ever served in Canada. . . ."[33]

In the police, Commissioner Irvine resigned early in 1886, accepting an appointment as an Indian Agent and eventually became the warden of Stony Mountain Penitentiary. His replacement, Lawrence W. Herchmer, a brother of the superintendent who accompanied Otter to Battleford, had not even served in the campaign but had acquired his experience as an Indian Agent in Manitoba. Inspector Dickens, the unhappy younger son of the novelist, also resigned soon after the rebellion and died a few months later.

For the survivors the campaign went on—the victors arguing with needless and unworthy violence about the correctness of their decisions and the courage of their exploits. Only the vanquished kept their silence. They had won every battle save the last.

Erindale College, July 1, 1972

Bibliographical Note

Much has been written about the events of 1885 in the North-West, a good deal of it by eye-witnesses. Such experiences, for most participants, comprised the most exciting and significant moments of their lives and their recollections reflect some of the partiality and partisanship which, perhaps inevitably, influenced their participation.

By 1886, the Dominion government had published reports by Middleton, Otter, Strange and other senior officers in a relatively carefully prepared volume, embellished with engraved maps and sketches (*Report Upon the Suppression of the Rebellion in the North- West Territories and Matters in Connection Therewith in 1885* (Canada, Sessional Papers, no. 6a, 1886). An abbreviated version in French was also published, a relative rarity for the time. Other reports by senior participants, including Major General Laurie and Lieutenant Colonel W. H. Jackson, also appeared in due course and precise expenditure for the campaign can be determined from the reports of the Auditor-General for 1885 and 1886.

To supplement the official reports and sometimes to contradict them, many leading participants rushed into print. Although written in haste to capitalize on a market, and with the obvious intention of casting a favourable light on both the government and General Middleton, Major C. A. Boulton's account of both the 1870 and the 1885 rebellions remains one of the most interesting and complete contemporary books on the North-West (*Reminiscences of the North-West Rebellions* (Toronto, Grip Printing, 1886). General Strange recalled his career and his many grievances in a spirited memoir (*Gunner Jingo's Jubilee* [London, Remington, 1893]). For the other side, Dumont's account of the events of 1885 was recorded by B. A. T. de Montigny (*Biographie et récit de Gabriel Dumont sur les évènements de 1885* [Montreal, n.p., 1889]). This account was later translated and published by G. F. G. Stanley ("Gabriel Dumont's Account of the North-West Rebellion, 1885," *Canadian Historical Review,* XXX, 3, September, 1949). Middleton's own account of the campaign originally appeared in serialized form in the United Service Magazine in 1893-4 but has since been published by another veteran of the campaign, the late Professor George H. Needler (*Suppression of Rebellion in the North-West Territories of Canada, 1885* [Toronto, University of Toronto Press, 1948]). William Cameron, a survivor of the Frog Lake killing and subsequently a prisoner of Big Bear, left memoirs which have appeared under two titles (*The War Trail of Big Bear* [Toronto, Ryerson Press, n.d.] and *Blood Red The Sun* [Toronto, Ryerson Press, 1952 4th ed.]).

A considerable body of pamphlet material and unpublished sources on the 1885 rebellion will be found in the Public Archives of Canada as well as in provincial archives in Manitoba, Saskatchewan and Alberta and at the Glenbow Foundation in Calgary. The papers of Lord Lansdowne, Lord Melgund (later the Earl of Minto), Sir John A. Macdonald, Edgar Dewdney and Sir Adolphe Caron are all available and the campaign diaries and other records of Colonel W. D. Otter have recently been added. Caron's papers are a particularly rich if ill-catalogued source. The author, in collaboration with Professor R. H. Roy of the University of Victoria and under the auspices of the Champlain Society, has published *Telegrams of the North-West Campaign, 1885*, based on material in the Caron Papers.

Among the more recent studies of the 1885 rebellion and its background, the pioneering work of G. F. G. Stanley in *The Birth of Western Canada*: *A History of the Riel Rebellions* (Toronto, University of Toronto Press, 1961 rev. ed.) and *Louis Riel* (Toronto, Ryerson, 1963) remains hardly challenged as a sober and sympathetic treatment of the Metis people and their leader, and of the events which led up to the two crises of 1870 and 1885. Other accounts, such as those of Joseph Kinsey Howard (*Strange Empire* [Toronto, Swan, 1970]) and E. B. Osler (*The Man Who Had to Hang* [Toronto, Longmans Green, 1961]) may be more gripping for a passing reader but, by throwing so brilliant a light on their heroes, both authors needlessly darken the rest of their story. Mention must be made of Pierre Berton's recent book on the construction of the Canadian Pacific Railway, for its graphic account of the hardships and endurance of the Canadian soldiers crossing the gaps in the line in the winter of 1885 (*The Last Spike*, [Toronto, McClelland & Stewart, 1971]).

Among recent contributors to the study of Riel and his time, the most accomplished is Hartwell Bowsfield of York University. His two books on Riel, *Louis Riel* (Toronto, Oxford, 1970) and *Louis Riel*: *Rebel of the Western Frontier or Victim of Politics and Prejudice* (Toronto, Copp Clark, 1969) will be of particular interest to students venturing into this field for the first time. There have also been some serious attempts to present the Indian side of the conflict, notably the pathfinding essay by W. B. Fraser ("Big Bear, Indian Patriot," *Alberta Historical Review*, XIV, 2, Spring, 1966) and Norma Sluman's book on Poundmaker (Toronto, Ryerson, 1967)

As in most fields of Canadian historiography, much remains to be done. In few are the pressures for myth-making so strong.

Notes

(Unless otherwise noted, all documentary sources refer to papers in the Public Archives of Canada. A more fully annotated account of the 1885 campaign may be found in the author's introduction in Morton and Roy, *The North-West Rebellion Telegrams. 1885* (Champlain Society, 1972).)

I. Duck Lake

1. B.A.T. de Montigny, *Biographie et récit de Gabriel Dumont sur les évènements de 1885* (Montreal, 1889) p. 125.
2. On the skirmish at Duck Lake, see G. F. G. Stanley, *The Birth of Western Canada* (Toronto, 1961, rev. ed.), pp. 327-8, 331-2; *Report of the Commissioner of the North West Mounted Police, 1885,* Canada, Sessional Papers, no. 8, 1886, pp. 38-9; de Montigny, *Dumont,* pp. 122-5.
3. On Riel and the Métis, see especially G. F. G. Stanley, *Louis Riel* (Toronto, 1963).
4. Macdonald to Dewdney, September 2, 1884, cited by L. H. Thomas, *The Struggle for Responsible Government in the North-West Territories, 1870-1897* (Toronto, 1956), p. 130.
5. Cited in Prince Albert *Times,* February 22, 1884, in *ibid.,* p. 123.
6. See W. J. C. Cherwinski, "Honoré Joseph Jaxon, Agitator, Disturber, Producer of Plans to Make Men Think, and Chronic Objector," *Canadian Historical Review,* XLVI, 2, January, 1965
7. See W. B. Fraser, "Big Bear: Indian Patriot," *Alberta Historical Review,* XIV, 2, Spring, 1966 (reprinted in Donald Swainson [ed.], *Historical Essays on the Prairie Provinces* [Toronto, 1970], pp. 71-88).
8. Dewdney to Macdonald, March 11, 1885, Macdonald Papers, vol. 107, p. 43010.
9. On Frog Lake, see W. B. Cameron, *The War Trail of Big Bear* (Boston, 1927), pp. 52-76; George Stanley (Mesunekwepan), "An Account of the Frog Lake Massacre," *Alberta Historical Review,* IV, 1, Winter, 1956.
10. Lansdowne to Derby, April 7, 1885, Lansdowne, Papers, A-623, p. 73.
11. Thomas White to Sir Charles Tupper, April 1, 1885, in E. M. Saunders (ed.), *The Life and Letters of the Hon. Sir Charles Tupper Bart., K.C.M.G.* (London, 1916), II, 51.

II. The Government Reacts

1. Dewdney to Macdonald, March 24, 1885, Dewdney Papers, vol. 3, pp. 1116-9. On Riel, see Stanley, *Western Canada,* pp. 311-2.
2. Macdonald to Dewdney, March 23, 1885, Dewdney Papers, vol. 3, p. 1105.

3. Hugh John Macdonald to Macdonald, June 8, 1884, Macdonald Papers, vol. 200, pp. 84653-4. On the military background, see C. P. Stacey, The Military Aspect of Canada's Winning of the West," *Canadian Historical Review*, XXI, 1, March, 1940.
4. Dewdney to Macdonald, March 22, 1885, Dewdney Papers, vol. 3, p. 1103.
5. Middleton to Melgund, March 24, 1885, Minto Papers, A-129.
6. Dewdney to Macdonald, March 25, 1885, Dewdney Papers, vol. 3, p. 1127. (Reports of a clash had appeared in the Toronto *Globe*, March 24, 1885.)
7. Cited in Desmond Morton, *Ministers and Generals* (Toronto, 1970), p. 139.
8. Montreal *Gazette*, March 25, 1885.
9. Middleton to Caron, March 27, 1885, Caron Papers, vol. 199, p. 16 (hereafter, N.W.R.T.).
10. Caron to Strange, March 29, 1885, *ibid.*, p. 44.
11. LaChapelle to Caron, March 28, 1885, Caron Papers, Vol. 192, p. 4798 (trans.).
12. R. Forsyth to Caron, April 4, 1885, *ibid.*, vol. 199, p. 176.
13. Anonymous to Caron, April 2, 1885, *ibid.*, p. 142 (trans.).
14. Robert Rumilly, *Histoire de la province de Québec*, vol. V, *Louis Riel* (Montreal, n.d.), p. 23.
15. Lt. Col. Frank Bond to Thomas White, April 2, 1885, Caron Papers, file 5714.
16. G. T. Denison, *Soldiering in Canada* (Toronto, 1900), pp. 265-6.
17. C. M. Douglas to Caron, March 31, 1885, N.W.R.T., p. 82.
18. Georges Beauregard, *Journal d'un militaire* (Québec, 1886), p. 15 (trans.).
19. Caron to Montizambert and Otter, March 31, 1885, N.W.R.T., pp. 70 and 81.
20. A.T.H. Williams to Caron, April 19, 1885, Caron Papers, vol. 192, p. 4910.
21. *Report of Lieut. Col. W. H. Jackson, Principal Supply, Pay and Transport Officer to the Northwest Forces and Chairman of the War Claims Commission on Matters in Connection with the Suppression of the Rebellion in the North-West Territories in 1885*, Canada, Sessional Papers, no. 9c, 1887, p. 6.
22. Joseph Royal to Caron, April 7, 1885, N.W.R.T., p. 204.
23. F. D. Barwick to Caron, April 6, 1885, *ibid.*, p. 202.
24. Wrigley to Caron, March 29, 1885, *ibid.*, p. 40.
25. Telegram enclosed with Smith to Macdonald, April 5, 1885, Macdonald Papers, vol. 106, p. 42414.
26. Caron to Wrigley, April 4, 1885, N.W.R.T., p. 145.
27. Amos Rowe to Mackenzie Bowell, April 13, 1885, *ibid.*, p. 263.
28. Wrigley to Caron, May 4, 1885, *ibid.*, p. 363.
29. Amyot to Caron, May 19, 1885, Caron Papers, vol. 192, p. 4784.

III. Fish Creek

1. Middleton to Caron, March 28, 1885, Caron Papers, vol. 192, p. 4784.
2. *Report Upon the Suppression of the Rebellion in the North-West Territories and Matters in Connection Therewith in 1885*, Canada, Sessional Papers, no 6a, p. 1 (hereafter, *Rebellion Report*).
3. Middleton to Caron, March 28, 1885, Caron Papers, vol. 192, p. 4784.
4. Middleton to Caron, April 8, 1885, N.W.R.T., p. 264.
5. Middleton to Caron, April 14, 1885 *ibid.*, p. 270.
6. Lansdowne to Macdonald, April 4, 1885, Lansdowne Papers, A-623, letterbook 2, p. 69.
7. Melgund to Lansdowne, April 3, 1885, Minto Papers, A-129.
8. Lansdowne to Melgund, April 6, 1885, *ibid.*
9. Macdonald to Middleton, March 29, 1885, Macdonald Papers, vol. 526, letterbook 23, pp. 142-5.
10. Fleming to Caron, April 15, 1885, N.W.R.T., p. 278.
11. Middleton to Caron, April 8, 1885, *ibid.*, p. 264.
12. Melgund's Diary, April 13, 1885, Minto Papers, A-129.
13. Middleton to Otter, April 11, 1885, Otter Papers.
14. Middleton to Caron, April 14, 1885, N.W.R.T., p. 270.

15. E. J. Chambers, *The Royal Grenadiers* (Toronto, 1904), p. 47.
16. Stanley, *Western Canada*, p. 356.
17. De Montigny *Dumont* p. 131.
18. On the battle, see C. A. Boulton, *Reminiscences of the North-West Rebellions etc.* (Toronto, 1886), pp. 224-36; Stanley, *Western Canada*, p. 359; *Rebellion Report*, pp. 17-20; Lt. Col. C. E. Long, "A Reminiscence of the North-West Campaign, 1885," *Canadian Defence Quarterly*, IV, 1, October, 1927, pp. 48-9; de Montigny, *Dumont*, pp. 130-134; Alexander Laidlaw, *From the St. Lawrence to the North Saskatchewan* .. (Halifax, 1886), pp. 22-5.
19. Melgund, "The Recent Rebellion in North-West Canada," *The Nineteenth Century*, XVIII, 2, June, 1885, p. 322.

IV. Batoche

1. Middleton to Duke of Cambridge, May 6, 1885, Royal Archives, Windsor Castle, Cambridge Papers.
2. Middleton to Caron, April 27, 1885, Caron Papers, vol., 192, pp. 4930-3.
3. Middleton to Caron, April 18, 1885, N.W.R.T., p. 329.
4. Middleton to Caron, April 27, 1885, Caron Papers, vol. 192, p. 4932.
5. Middleton to Cambridge, May 6, 1885, Cambridge Papers.
6. Middleton to Caron, May 1, 1885, N.W.R.T., p. 346 (See Toronto *Globe*, April 21 and 28 and May 2, 1885).
7. Caron to Wrigley, May 2, 1885, N.W.R.T., pp. 348-9.
8. G. H. Needler (ed.), *Suppression of the Rebellion in the North-West Territories of Canada, 1885* (Toronto, 1948), p. 27.
9. *Report of Major General J. W. Laurie, Commanding Base and Lines of Communication, Upon Matters in Connection with the Suppression of the Rebellion in the North-West Territories,* Canada, Sessional Papers, no. 9d, 1887, pp. 9-10, 24-9.
10. Caron to Middleton, May 7, 1885, N.W.R.T., p. 375.
11. *Rebellion Report*, pp. 39-41 (Major Smith's report).
12. Orton to Caron, September 10, 1885, Caron Papers, vol. 193, p. 5348; Toronto *Mail*, January 29, 1886.
13. Middleton to Cambridge, May 6, 1885, Cambridge Papers.
14. Melgund's Diary, May 9, 1885.
15. Lansdowne to Derby, May 11, 1885, Derby Papers, A-32.
16. *Rebellion Report*, p. 30
17. Middleton to Caron, May 11, 1885, N.W.R.T., p. 405.
18. On the attack, see *Rebellion Report*, pp. 32-3; Boulton, *Reminiscences*, pp. 279-285. On responsibility for launching the attack, see the explanation by Stanley, *Western Canada*, p. 449n.
19. C. A. Boulton to Lt. Col. D'Arcy Boulton, May 25, 1885, Macdonald Papers, vol. 106, p. 42479.
20. Quoted in Middleton to Caron, May 12, 1885, N.W.R.T., p. 419.

V. Cut Knife Hill

1. Crowfoot to Macdonald, April 11, 1885, Macdonald Papers, vol. 106, p. 42426.
2. Middleton to Otter, April 11, 1885, Otter Papers.
3. Otter to Dewdney, April 26, 1885, Dewdney Papers, vol. 5, p. 1806.
4. Middleton to Otter, April 26, 1885, Otter Papers.
5. Dewdney to Otter, April 26, 1885, Dewdney Papers, vol. 5, p. 1807.
6. Cited in G. H. Needler, *Louis Riel* (Toronto, 1956), p. 37.
7. On the battle, see *Rebellion Report*, pp. 23-5; *Report of the Commissioner of the N.W.M.P., 1885,* pp. 52-3; O. C. C. Pelletier, *Mémoires, souvenirs de famille et récits* (Quebec, 1940), pp. 231ff; Boulton, *Reminiscences*, pp. 312-22.

8. Middleton to Otter, May 1, 1885, Otter Papers.
9. Middleton to Caron, May 5, 1885, N.W.R.T., p. 368.
10. Middleton to Caron, May 6, 1885, *ibid.*, p. 371.

VI. Frenchman's Butte

1. John Cottingham to Caron, April 5, 1885, N.W.R.T., pp. 167-8.
2. T. B. Strange, *Gunner Jingo's Jubilee* (London, 1896), pp. 386.
3. Strange to Dewdney, April 10, 1885, Dewdney Papers, vol. 7, p. 2529.
4. Middleton to Cambridge, May 6, 1885, Cambridge Papers.
5. Middleton to Caron, April 27, 1885, Caron Papers, vol. 192, pp. 4932-3.
6. Strange, *Gunner Jingo,* p. 432.
7. C. E. Denny to Dewdney, April 24, 1885, Dewdney Papers, vol. 2, pp. 509ff.
8. Dewdney to Denny, April 21, 1885, *ibid.*, p. 501.
9. Middleton to Caron, April 29, 1885, Caron Papers, vol. 192, p. 4934.
10. *Rebellion Report,* p. 55.
11. *Ibid.,* p. 55.
12. Caron to Amyot, April 21, 1885, N.W.R.T., p. 298.
13. Amyot to Caron, May 14, 1885, *ibid.*, p. 416.
14. Amyot to Caron, May 18, 1885, *ibid.*, pp. 443-4.
15. Canada, House of Commons, *Debates,* February 25, 1889, p. 327.
16. *Rebellion Report,* p. 55.
17. Strange, *Gunner Jingo,* p. 492.
18. On the battle, see *ibid.*, pp. 489-92; *Rebellion Report,* pp. 55-9; C. R. Daoust, *Cent-vingt jours de service actif, récit historique très complet de la campagne du 65e au Nord-ouest* (Montreal, 1886), p. 91; S. B. Steele, *Forty Years in Canada* (Toronto, 1915), pp. 222-223.
19. Steel, *Forty Years,* pp. 224-5.

VII. Capturing Big Bear

1. Middleton to Caron, May 14, 1885, N.W.R.T., pp. 446-7.
2. *Rebellion Report.*
3. John G. Donkin, *Trooper and Redskin in the Far North-West* (London, 1889), p. 148.
4. *Rebellion Report,* p. 6.
5. *Ibid.,* p. 6.
6. D. J. Goodspeed, *Battle Royal: A History of the Royal Regiment of Canada, 1862-1962* (Toronto, 1962), p. 54.
7. Strange to Elinor Strange, n.d., in E. Strange to Caron, June 2, 1885, Caron Papers, vol. 193, p. 5199.
8. *Ibid.*
9. Steel, *Forty Years,* p. 228.
10. Anon. *Reminiscences of a Bungle by one of the Bunglers* (Toronto, 1887), p. 48.
11. C. W. Alison to Edward Blake, n.d., Ontario Archives, Blake Papers, II, 6, envelope 14.
12. R. H. Roy, "Rifleman Forin in the Riel Rebellion", *Saskatchewan History,* XXI, 3 Autumn, 1968, p. 107.
13. W. R. Oswald to Caron, May 31, 1885, Caron Papers, file 6012.
14. P. D. Hughes to Caron, June 27, 1885, *ibid.*, file 6179.
15. *Illustrated War News* (Toronto), May 21, 1885.
16. Charles A. Bossé to [indeciperable], June 20, 1885, Caron Papers, vol. 193, pp. 5171-2.
17. Whitehead to Caron, May 24, 1885, N.W.R.T., pp. 471-2.
18. Caron to Wrigley, May 22, 1885, *ibid.*, p. 463.
19. Middleton to Caron, May 22, 1885, *ibid.*, p. 464.
20. Whitehead to Caron, June 8, 1885, Caron Papers, file 5869.
21. Middleton to Caron, June 21, 1885, N.W.R.T., p. 525.

22. Caron to Middleton, June 30, 1885, *ibid.,* p. 547.
23. Williams to Caron, April 29, 1885, Caron Papers, file 5321.
24. Amyot to Caron, July 11, 1885, N.W.R.T., p. 570.

VIII. The Execution of Louis Riel

1. Middleton to Caron, June 23, 1885, N.W.R.T., pp. 529-30.
2. Dewdney to Macdonald, June 23, 1885, Macdonald Papers, vol. 107, p. 43170.
3. House of Commons, *Debates,* July 17, 1885, p. 3469.
4. Manitoba *Free Press,* August 12, 1885.
5. J. H. Metcalfe to Caron, August 10, 1885, Caron Papers, file 6611.
6. Metcalfe to Caron, June 2, 1885, *ibid.,* file 5565.
7. Caron to William Clark, August 1, 1885, N.W.R.T., p. 607.
8. Caron to Jackson, August 21, 1885, Caron Papers, letterbook 13, pp. 125-6.
9. George Hatton to Caron, February 8, 1886, *ibid.,* file 9918.
10. William Boyle to Caron, November 25, 1885, *ibid.,* file 7672.
11. *Rebellion Report,* p. 289.
12. *Ibid.,* pp. 182, 186.
13. *Ibid.,* pp. 68-9.
14. *Militia General Orders,* no. 14, July 9, 1885.
15. Stanley to Lansdowne, July 22, 1885, Public Record Office, London C.O. 42/780, pp. 395-6.
16. Lansdowne to Stanley, July 10, 1886, C.O. 42/781, p. 67.
17. War Office to Colonial Office, February 5, 1886, C.O. 42/785, p. 206.
18. Lansdowne to Macdonald, July 28, 1885, Lansdowne Papers, A-623, letterbook 2, p. 210.
19. Needler, *Louis Riel,* p. 5.
20 Orton to Caron, September 10, 1885, Caron Papers, vol. 193, p. 5350.
21. *Reminiscences of a Bungle,* p. 44.
21. C. E. Panet to Otter, December 11, 1885, Otter Papers.
23. *The Queen vs. Louis Riel, Accused and Convicted of the Crime of High Treason ....* (Queen's Printer, Ottawa, 1886).
24. H. A. Ward to Macdonald, August 26, 1885, Macdonald Papers, vol. 108, p. 43418.
25. Henry O'Brien to Macdonald, August 21, 1885 and note, *ibid.,* pp. 43374-6.
26. Stanley, *Western Canada,* p. 396.
27. Lacombe memorandum, n.d. (July, 1885), Macdonald Papers, vol. 107, p. 43240.
28. Jean Larmour, "Edgar Dewdney and the Aftermath of the Rebellion," *Saskatchewan History,* XXIII, 4, Autumn, 1970.
29. Caron to Middleton, June 12, 1885, N.W.R.T., p. 506.
30. Middleton to Caron, June 15, 1885, *ibid.,* p. 512.
31. *Report of the Select Committee in re Charles Bremner's Furs,* Canada, Sessional Papers, Appendix No. 1, 1890.
32. Caron to Lt. Col. G. S. Maunsell, September 30, 1885, Caron Papers, letterbook 34, p. 55.
33. Strange to Macdonald, August 28, 1885, Macdonald Papers, vol. 85, p. 33208.

The Order of Battle

North-West Field Force
1885

Batoche Column
Commander—Major-General Frederick Middleton
Chief of Staff—Lord Melgund
Commanding Artillery—Lieut.-Col. C. E. Montizambert
Commanding Infantry—Lieut.-Col. Bowen van Straubenzie
Deputy Adjutant-General—Lieut.-Col. C. F. Houghton
Acting Quartermaster General—Captain H. de H. Haig R.E.
Chief Transport Officer—S. L. Bedson

* "A" Battery, Regiment of Canadian Artillery (Quebec)
  Lieut.-Col. C. E. Montizambert (4-107)†
* Winnipeg Field Battery (Winnipeg) Major E. W. Jarvis (3-59)
* Detachment of "C" Company, Infantry School Corps (Toronto)
  Major Henry Smith (2-40)
* 10th Royal Grenadiers (Toronto) Lieut.-Col. H. J. Grasett (17-250)
  Midland Battalion (Belleville, Lindsay, Port Hope, Kingston)
  Lieut.-Col. A. T. H. Williams M.P. (34-342)
* 90th Battalion of Rifles (Winnipeg) Lieut.-Col. Alfred
  Mackeand (29-298)
* Boulton's Mounted Infantry (Russell and Birtle, Man.,)
  Major C. A. Boulton (5-108)
* French's Scouts (around Qu'Appelle) Captain John French (2-33)
  Dominion Land Surveyors' Intelligence Corps (Ottawa)
  Captain J. S. Dennis (1936).

* At Fish Creek
† Strength in officers and other ranks.

Battleford Column
Commander—Lieut.-Col. W. D. Otter
Chief of Staff—Superintendent W. M. Herchmer
Brigade Major—Lieutenant J. W. Sears
Brigade Quartermaster—Captain G. W. Mutton
Brigade Transport Officer—George B. Murphy

"B" Battery, Regiment of Canadian Artillery (Kingston)
   Major C. J. Short (8-106)
North-West Mounted Police (Regina) Superintendent L. R. Neale
   (1-50) and garrisons from Fort Pitt and Battleford (2-41)
Queen's Own Rifles (Toronto) Lieut.-Col. A. A. Miller (18-257)
Detachment of "C" Company, Infantry School Corps (Toronto)
   Lieutenant R. L. Wadmore (1-50)
Governor General's Foot Guards sharpshooters (Ottawa)
   Captain A. H. Todd (3-48)
Battleford Rifles (Battleford) Captain E. A. Nash (3-42)

Alberta Field Force
Commander—Major-General T. B. Strange
Brigade Major—Major Alfred Dale
Assistant Quartermaster General—Captain Edward Palliser
Transport and Supply Officer—H. Hamilton

Steele's Scouts (including North-West Mounted Police) Major S. B.
   Steele (5-84)
65th Mount Royal Rifles (Montreal) Lieut.-Col. J. Alderic Ouimet
   M.P. (23-317)
Winnipeg Light Infantry (Winnipeg) Lieut.-Col. Osborne Smith
   (29-298)

Headquarters at Winnipeg
Principal Supply Officer and Paymaster—Lieut.-Col. W. H. Jackson
Chief Transport Officer—Lieut.-Col. E. A. Whitehead
Paymaster—Major George Guy

Headquarters at Swift Current   (moved to Moose Jaw)
Commanding Lines of Communications—Major-General J.
   Wimburn Laurie
Deputy Surgeon-General—T. G. Roddick M.D.
Purveyor-General—Senator Michael Sullivan M.D.

Militia on the Lines of Communication

Touchwood Hills:
Cavalry School Corps (Quebec) Lieut.-Col. J. F. Turnbull (3-45)

Humboldt:
Governor General's Body Guard (Toronto) Lieut.-Col. G. T.
  Denison (8-73)
York and Simcoe Rangers formed from 12th and 35th Battalions)
  Lieut.-Col. W. E. O'Brien M.P. (27-342)

Clarke's Crossing:
7th Fusiliers (London) Lieut.-Col. W. de la Ray Williams (20-237)

Calgary and Vicinity:
9th Voltigeurs (Quebec) Lieut.-Col. G. A. Amyot M.P. (28-204)

Regina:
Montreal Garrison Artillery (Montreal) Lieut.-Col. W. R. Oswald
  (20-276)

Qu'Appelle:
Winnipeg Troop of Cavalry (Winnipeg) Capt. Cornelius
  Knight (1-35)
Winnipeg Battalion of Infantry (Winnipeg) Lieut-Col. Thomas
  Scott M.P. (24-408)

McLeod and Lethbridge:
Rocky Mountain Rangers (Southern Alberta) Major John
  Stewart (7-57)

Yorkton:
Yorkton Militia Corps (Yorkton) Major T. Charles Watson (1-63)

Along the C.P.R. line:
Halifax Provisional Battalion (Halifax) Lieut.-Col. J. J. Bremner
  (32-349)

Index